D0618629

As Far
As I Can
See

As Far As I Can See

*Contemporary Writing
of the Middle Plains*

Edited with Introductions
by
Charles L. Woodard

Associate Editor for Production
Ted Kooser

Illustrations by Robert L. Hanna

WINDFLOWER PRESS
Post Office Box 82213
Lincoln, NE 68501

Published in the United States of America
by Windflower Press
P. O. Box 82213
Lincoln, NE 68501

Printed in the United States of America
Cover design by Patrick Ervin
Illustrations by Robert L. Hanna

Second Printing
10 9 8 7 6 5 4 3 2

ISBN: 0-931534-11-9

for Laura, Ryan, Andrea

To Scythe Press, for "On Warm Summer Nights" by David Bengston. To *Calliope*, for "Hands" by Shirley Buettner. To Juniper Press, for "Before Owls Sleep," from *Walking Out the Dark* by Shirley Buettner. To *Blackjack*, for "Burning" by Shirley Buettner. "In Cottonwood Township" by Shirley Buettner is reprinted from *Prairie Schooner*, by permission of University of Nebraska Press; copyright ©1986 by University of Nebraska Press. To *Kansas Quarterly* for "Village Softball League" by Shirley Buettner; copyright ©1983 by *Kansas Quarterly*. To *Abraxas* for "The Swiss Chalet Barometer" by Shirley Buettner. To *Platte Valley Review* for "Rising From This Flat Land" by Shirley Buettner. To *Poets On:* for "The Cottonwood" by Shirley Buettner. To Robert Bly, for "Three Kinds of Pleasures," "Hunting Pheasants in a Cornfield," "Sunset at a Lake," "Fall," "Approaching Winter," "Driving Toward the Lac Qui Parle River," and "A Man Writes to a Part of Himself," all from *Silence in the Snowy Fields*, copyright ©1960, 1961, 1962 by Robert Bly, printed with his permission. To Carnegie-Mellon University Press for "Neighbor in May" by Michael Dennis Browne, from *Smoke From the Fires*. To *The New Yorker*, for "Handicapped Children Swimming" by Michael Dennis Browne. "Field Work" by Douglas Cockrell, first appeared in *Poetspeak: In Their Work, About Their Work*, edited by Paul B. Janeczko, published by Bradbury Press, Inc. Reprinted by permission of the editor and the publisher. To *Oakwood*, for Doug Cockrell's "Dakota Town." To Victor Contoski, for "All Souls," from *A Kansas Sequence*, published by Cottonwood/Tellus. To Blue Cloud Quarterly Press, for permission to reprint "Grandfather at the Indian Health Clinic" by Elizabeth Cook-Lynn. To Vantage Press for permission to reprint "The Bare Facts" by Elizabeth Cook-Lynn, from *Then Badger Said This*. To *Friend's Journal*, for "Smoke" by Bruce Cutler. "Divorce Court," by Phil Dacey, is reprinted from *Prairie Schooner*, by permission of University of Nebraska Press. Copyright ©1987 by University of Nebraska Press. To Florence Dacey for "Composting"; prior publication by Kraken Press and Minnesota Writers' Publishing House. To Phil Dacey, for "Looking at Models in the Sears Catalogue," from *How I Escaped From the Labyrinth and Other Poems*, Carnegie-Mellon University Press, 1977. To Spoon River Poetry Press for "The Auction" and "One Summer Afternoon" by Leo Dangel, from *Old Man Brunner Country*. To *Mid-American Review*, for "Passing On Through Faith" by Gary David. To Ahsahta Press, for "Grazing Cattle" by Susan Deal, from *The Dark is a Door*, copyright ©1984 by Ahsahta Press, Boise State University. To Milkweed Editions, for "Pasttime" by Emilio DeGrazia, from *This Sporting Life*. To Riverfront and Free Rein Press for "Babicka's Funeral" by Lorraine Duggin. To *South Dakota Review* for "A Love Letter" by David Dwyer. To *Horizons: The South Dakota Writers Anthology*, for

David Dwyer's "Baling Wheatstraw on My 33rd Birthday." To Henry Holt and Company, for "The Red Convertible" by Louise Erdrich; copyright ©1984 by Lousie Erdrich. Reprinted by permission of Henry Holt and Company, Inc.. To Holt Rinehart Winston for permission to reprint "Indian Boarding School; The Runaways" from *Jacklight*, Copyright © 1984 by Louise Erdrich. " To Harper & Row, Publishers, for "Flyway and "Blizzard" from *Cold Stars and Fireflies* by Barbara Juster Esbensen. (Thomas Y. Crowell). Copyright ©1984 by Barbara Juster Esbensen. Reprinted by permission of Harper & Row, Publishers, Inc.. To Harper & Row, Publishers, for "Wolf" from *Words With Wrinkled Knees* by Barbara Juster Esbensen. (Thomas Y., Crowell). Copyright ©1986 by Barbara Juster Esbensen. Reprinted by permission of Harper & Row, Publishers, Inc.. To *South Dakota Review*, for "Winter Kill" by David Allan Evans. To Plains Press, for "The Junkman" by David Allan Evans. "Pigeons" by David Allan Evans is reprinted with permission from *Religion & Public Education*. "The Touchdown in Slow Motion," Copyright © 1969 by Washington & Lee University, reprinted from *Shenandoah: The Washington & Lee University Review*, with the permission of the editor. To *Esquire*, for "Pole Vaulter" by David Allan Evans. To *Poetry Northwest*, for "Deer on Cars" by David Allan Evans. To *Kansas Quarterly*, for "Football" by David Allan Evans, Copyright © 1973 by *Kansas Quarterly*. To *Plainsong*, for "Rakers" by David Allan Evans. To *Southern Humanities Review*, for "Wasps" by Steve Hahn. To Ron Hansen for "Nebraska." To Seven Buffalos Press, for "Hands" by Linda Hasselstrom, from *From Seedbed to Harvest*. To Spoon River Poetry Press, for "Clara: In the Post Office," from *Roadkill* by Linda Hasselstrom. To *North Country Anvil*, for Linda Hasselstrom's "Now I Know Grouse." To Prairie Gate Press, for "Letting the Wind Talk" by Tom Hennen. And to Tom Hennen, for "Minneapolis," from *The Heron With No Business Sense*, Minnesota Writers Publishing House. To Jim Heynen, for "Custer Cafe Eat," from *Notes From Custer*, Bear Claw Press. To *Yarrow*, for Larry Holland's "Could You Have Blinked And Not Seen It And Been Saved?" To Milkweed Editions for permission to reprint Bill Holm's two boxelder poems, and to Plains Press and Saybrook Publishers for permission to reprint "Horizontal Grandeur" by Bill Holm, from *Prairie Days*. To *Poetry East*, for "Walking Through a Wall" by Louis Jenkins. To *The Chariton Review*, for "Appointed Rounds" by Louis Jenkins. To New Rivers Press, for "Swans" by Deborah Keenan, from *The Only Window That Counts*. To Robert King, for "Pioneer Cemetery," from *Standing Around Outside*, Bloodroot Press. To *Elkhorn Review*, for "Bicycle" by Greg Kosmicki. To Viking Press, for Greg Kuzma's "The Insurance Men," from *Good News*. To Basilisk Press, for "If I Ran the World," from *The Buffalo Shoot*, by Greg Kuzma. To BookMark Press, for

Denise Low's "Looking ForYour Blue Spot," from *Dragon Kite*. To University of Kansas Natural Histories Press, for "Rolla to Lawrence" and "Clinton River Displacement" by Denise Low, from *Spring Geese and Other Poems*. To Frederick Manfred for permission to reprint the exerpts from his books, *Conquering Horse, Lord Grizzly*, and *The Golden Bowl*. To Overlook Press, for "Wedding Song" by Freya Manfred, from *American Roads*. published by The Overlook Press, Lewis Hollow Road, Woodstock, NY. To The Ohio University Press, Athens, for "The Roads into the Country" and "Such Lies They Told Us" by Thomas McGrath, from *The Movie at the End of the World*, Swallow Press, 1972. Reprinted with the permission of Swallow/Ohio University Press. To *Mid American Review*, for "The Wide Receiver" by Bill Meissner. To *The Indiana Review*, for "The Outfielder" by Bill Meissner. To Ohio University Press, for "Drawing Swastikas," "Sunday Afternoon Drive," and "Learning to Breathe Underwater" by Bill Meissner, from *The Sleepwalker's Son*. To *Great River Review*, for "Not Much Unsettled or Disturbed" by Kent Meyers. To *Minnesota Monthly* for permission to reprint "Windbreak" by Kent Meyers. "Inheritance" is reprinted from *The Middle of the World* by Kathleen Norris by permission of the University of Pittsburgh Press. ©1981 by Kathleen Norris. To *The Madison Review*, for "In the Fresh Air" by Anthony Oldknow. To *Plains Poetry Journal*, for "Gathering" by Anthony Oldknow. To *Luna Tack*, for "We Cannot Save Him" by Lon Otto. To *Writer's Premiere*, for "Cardinal Rules" by Nancy Paddock. To *Sou'wester*, for "Estate Sale" by Nancy Paddock. To Milkweed Editions, for "Our First Generation of Old Men" and "Frogs" by Joe Paddock, from *Earth Tongues*. To Joe Paddock for permission to reprint "Grandfather Sonnenberg" from *A Song Like My Own*, published by the Southwest Minnesota Arts and Humanities Council. To Puerto Del Sol for "Winter Tree" by Nancy Peters. "Carnivore" by John Calvin Rezmerski is reprinted from *Held For Questioning* by permission of the University of Missouri Press. Copyright © by John Calvin Rezmerski. To *Poetry Northwest*, for "July" by Richard Robbins. "Land" by Bob Ross is reprinted from *Prairie Schooner* by permission of University of Nebraska Press. Copyright © 1978 by University of Nebraska Press. To Milkweed Editions, for Ruth Roston's "Symptoms," from *Minnesota Writers: Poetry*. To New Rivers Press, for "The Dream Collector" by Ruth Roston, from *I Live in the Watchmaker's Town*. To *Columbia Magazine of the Arts*, for "Photo of Women Plowing" by CarolAnn Russell. "Keeping the Horses" is reprinted from *Pointing Out the Sky* (Sandhills Press, 1985), Copyright © 1985 by Roy Scheele. "A Burial, Green" is reprinted from *The Night Won't Save Anyone, Poems* by Marcia Southwick, © 1980 by the University of Georgia Press. Reprinted by permission of the University of Georgia Press. "Memorial Day" and "Early

Snow" by Carlee Swann are reprinted from *The Hadley Poems,* published by Verna Knott. "Dane Church Standing Empty Outside Red Cloud" by Kris Vervaecke is reprinted from *Forty Nebraska Poets,* edited by Greg Kuzma, The Best Cellar Press. "Deserted Farm," "Line Storm," and "Valley of the Kaw" by Mark Vinz are reprinted from *Winter Promises* from BkMk Press. "At the Vietnam Memorial" by Cary Waterman, first appeared in Vol. 29, No.1 of *The Literary Review.* "Klein's Amusement Show," by Cary Waterman, is from *First Thaw,* Minnesota Writers Publishing House, 1975. "Neighbor," by Charles Waterman, is reprinted from *Northeast.* Copyright © *Northeast* and Juniper Press. To *The Small Farm,* for "Driving Home" by Don Welch. To Kearney State College Press, for "Baltimore Oriole" by Don Welch, from *The Rarer Game.* To Copper Canyon Press, for "Hollyhocks" by Kathleene West, from *Landbound,* 1978. To *South Dakota Review,* for "Recovery" by Kevin Woster. To *Dakota Arts Quarterly,* for "In the Center of It" by Kevin Woster.

The introductions to these pages quote from a number of sources. We acknowledge *The Tennessee Poetry Journal* for William Stafford's remarks about regionalism. The William Faulkner quotation is from "William Faulkner; An Interview" from *William Faulkner: Three Decades of Criticism,* edited by Frederick J. Hoffman and Olga W. Vickery (New York: Harcourt, Brace and World, Inc. 1960). We acknowledge Kathleen Norris for the use of the title of her poem from *The Middle of the World:* University of Pittsburgh Press, Pittsburgh, Pennsylvania, 1981. The Scott Momaday quotations are from *The Names: A Memoir* (New York: Harper & Row, 1976) and *The World of the American Indian,* edited by Jules B. Billard (Washington: National Geographic Society, 1975). We thank Utah State University Press for permission to reprint "Morning of the Wolf" by Keith Wilson. Douglas Worth's poem in the introduction to our "Getting Physical" section is from *Invisibilities* (Cambridge, Massachusetts: Apple-wood Press, 1977). In our "The Wild and the Tame" section, the quotation from Luther Standing Bear is from his *Land of the Spotted Eagle* (Boston and New York: Houghton Mifflin Co., 1933). The John Dos Passos quote was discovered in *Of Discovery and Destiny: An Anthology of American Writers* (Golden, Colorado: Fulcrum, Inc., 1986). The Paul Shepard quotation is from "Place in American Culture" from the Fall, 1977 issue of *The North American Review.* The "grain of sand" quotation from William Blake can be found in *Auguries of Innocence.* And finally, the Chippewa quotation is translated from the Chippewa by Francis Densmore, in *Chippewa Music II,* Bureau of American Ethnology, Bulletin 53, 1913.

To Robert L. Hanna and the University of Nebraska Press for permission to reprint several illustrations from *Sketches of Nebraska*. The other illustrations appear here for the first time.

Our special thanks to Doug Cockrell for giving us the title of this book.

CONTENTS

CONTENTS

Introduction

T here is a tendency to undervalue the local and the familiar. Sometimes, as the saying goes, familiarity even "breeds contempt." Maybe that is why "art" is often thought of as something which happens elsewhere, in places and times which seem more exotic and interesting. That thinking seems especially true of less populated places like the Midwest, whose people have usually looked to the coasts, especially to the east, for models of "American" art.

Yet the poet William Stafford believes that all experience, and therefore all art, is "local, somewhere." And William Faulkner, after artistic beginnings which were mostly distant from his place, turned in his writing to his own Jefferson County, Mississippi, and wrote out of that place for most of the rest of his life. He called it "my own little postage stamp of native soil." *Because* his novels were so specifically, energetically, passionately about his place, they were also about everywhere else.

That kind of writing has been created for decades on the Great Plains, and the volume of it has multiplied rapidly in recent years. Across this prairie landscape, in places like the Dakotas, Minnesota, Nebraska, Kansas—the middle of the area which the poet Kathleen Norris refers to as "the middle of the world"—significant literature is being written. Native American writer N. Scott Momaday says: "Events do indeed take place; they have meaning in relation to the things around them." The writers in this book demonstrate the importance of that idea. They are inspired by these plains to create works with universal implications.

Consider the thematically arranged sections which follow. Each includes explorations of relationship and relationship possibilities, and the land is central to all of them. In "Legacy and Loss," traditional values, which naturally include relationships with the earth, are compared and contrasted with current ways of being. In "Each to Each," the natural world is both a relationship possibility and frequently the environment for exploring human interactions, and "Getting Physical" examines the human need for a muscular response to creation. The last two sections, "The Wild and the Tame" and "Letting the Wind Talk," contrast the effects of being insensitive to the environment with the benefits of earth knowledge. Of course, there are multiple "themes"—which is to say implications and ideas—in most good pieces of writing, and each work included here contains several important discussion possibilities. But the idea of relationship with the earth is dominant in Midwestern literature, and the structure of this book is a logical consequence of that fact.

Because there are so many midwesterners writing energetically in the genre of poetry these days, there are many poems in this volume. These are written in a rich variety of forms, but they have

many elements in common. All good poetry features artful combina-
tions of the right words, bright original images, creative comparisons,
and stimulating mystery.   All good poetry also finds ways to emphasize human voices, because the sounds a poem makes are of primary
importance.   Listening is the first step on the way to whatever learning
is involved.

Some poems, however, use regular rhyme and meter formulas
as the main method for delivering the voice or voices the poet wants the
reader to hear. Artfully used, rhyme and meter can create powerful
effects.   But other writers have other main ways of emphasizing their
voices.   They use techniques such as   irregular rhyme and meter,
word and sound repetitions, line length contrasts, contrasting levels of
diction, and punctuation variety.   Those methods also emphasize
their voices and therefore humanize their poems. In short, there are
many patterns of expression, many ways of voicing life. Well-written
"free verse" is as much an artful calculation of effect as is well-written
poetry which rhymes.

Finally, how should "literature" be read?   The contemporary
world tends to condition us to approach what we read in a singular way,
looking for precise and exact meanings.   That approach can be pro-
ductive in dealing with data-based subject matter where "right answers" are involved. But literature, especially poetry, resists such
analysis. Mystery lives at the center of a good poem, as it lives creatively
at the center of our lives, stimulating us to think, and think again. "What
is the poet trying to say?" can be a very reductive question, if it leads to
a prose paragraph summary of the poem which excludes other possibilities. The poet is not a person incapable of direct statement, just as the
painter is not someone who paints because she cannot frame an ex-
planatory paragraph. Rather, the poet is "trying" to present the wonderful complexity of experience, trying to record and respond and
suggest and explore. Within the artful construct which is the creatively
evocative poem, there can be at least as many "poems" as there are
readers willing to apply their unique experiences to what they read.

Which is not to suggest that a work of literature means anything anyone says it means.   It is certainly possible to misunderstand
the basic meanings of words, and to lack the experience needed to
understand some of a work's images and allusions.   The value of "dis-
cussing" literature is that we can, out of the unique experiences which
are our individual lives, help each other.   We can dissolve misunder-
standings and suggest "meanings" which deepen each others' under-
standings of the beautifully informative life which literature
presents.   This anthology is a contribution to that necessary and
perhaps most valuable discussion.

Legacy and Loss

S hakespeare began his Sonnet 64 with these words:

> *When I have seen by time's fell hand defaced*
> *The rich-proud cost of outworn buried age*

In those lines and throughout his poem, Shakespeare described the sad signs of change. He saw structures decay and fall, and he realized that even the earth is worn away through time. Recognizing the effects of time on what he observed, Shakespeare had to accept what time would mean to him. "Time will come," he wrote, "and take my love away." Loss is inevitable.

Wordsworth also examined the consequences of time in his "Ode":

> *It is not now as it hath been of yore—*
> *Turn whereso'er I may,*
> *By night or day,*
> *The things which I have seen I now can see no more.*

Yet later in that same poem, Wordsworth described the comfort he found in the beauty of what had been, and in what was left:

> *What though the radiance which was once so bright*
> *Be now forever taken from my sight,*
> *Though nothing can bring back the hour*
> *Of splendor in the grass, or glory in the flower;*
> *We will grieve not, rather find*
> *Strength in what remains behind.*

Wordsworth was, finally, reconciled to change, and determined to use his knowledge of the past in a positive way. He valued his legacy.

These two themes, of legacy and loss, are dominant in the contemporary literature of the Great Plains. Writers regret the many dramatic changes which have occurred in the recent history of these prairie places, and they regret their personal losses, but they also record and sometimes even celebrate the physical and spiritual legacies which remain. As is the case with Wordsworth's poem, often both themes are contained in the same work.

This section begins with "In Cottonwood Township," a poem about the gradual loss of community in a rural township. Here the poet does what many writers do so well: she sees larger meanings in the details of the world. Through telling details—loosening thread, floating milkweed fluff and specks of dust, flying geese, burning weeds, the departure of a daughter—she records and regrets the larger loss of her rural community.

In contrast, the writer of "Telling Childhood" sees in the emblem of the present—the shopping mall—signs of what has been. He sees the energetic, physical, natural past against the synthetic present. His contrasting of the waterfall "down artificial rock" in the mall with the vivid natural past he remembers is of course irony—a frequent device of the creative writer. Water, the most spontaneous, energetic, and creative force in a natural environment, is mechanically displayed in his mall scene to demonstrate the ironic contrast between the present and the past.

In the eight poems which follow , other rural community losses are recorded. These poems are together a panorama of images of the past surrendering to the present: a diminished Dakota town, the remnants of a Nebraska roundhouse, an empty church, deserted farms, an industrialized valley, an abandoned cemetery. These scenes measure distances in time and attitude. They are visions of change.

Then the focus shifts to personal loss. "After School" and "At the Vietnam Memorial" are poems about the deaths of schoolmates in war, while "Last Summer and the One Before" and "Could You Have Blinked And Not Seen It And Been Saved?" describe the deaths of the fathers of young children—one by accident and the other apparently by suicide. Finally, in "The Dream Collector," the poet sees in the losses she observes her own inevitable end. As butterflies die, and against the losses of childhood and of lovers, "her own death shimmers."

But despite such inevitabilities, some contemporary writers find the kind of hope Wordsworth found. For example, in "Neighbors in May," the grieving husband "dreams of repairing the damage." He *imagines* his recovery. And in "Babicka's Funeral" and "Inheritance," the poets see in the lives and deaths of the mother and the grandmother they loved some resources for their own lives. Similarly, "Grandfather Sonnenberg" is a celebration of a life lived so courageously that it inspires its inheritors. And in "The Gift," the poet is moved by the image of his dying father to envision a more hopeful future in a very powerful way. "Dreaming growth," he "sees" the seed, the symbol of rebirth and hope. In all of these poems, imagination—whether of the past, the present, or the future—is central.

The next several poems are demonstrations of how important language is to the process of imagining. In "Pigeons of My Youth," the poet's past is present through his vivid multi-sensory recollection of those bright birds. "They never give up" not only because feeding pigeons are so persistent, but also because the poet's language is so *in*sistent, as he re-creates his past in the present tense. Similarly, the stories in the two poems which are next, "Our First Generation of Old Men" and "Frogs," are carried forward into the present by energetic language, and their events recur as the poems unfold. As the poet says at the end of "Frogs," these are "stories you learn early and carry with you." They are resources. And the next poem, "Ritual," is in many ways a summary of the legacy of the creatively re-told past. It is also a statement of acceptance of what has been and will be.

The final work in the section, "Estate Sale," is also a story, a story of affirmation, continuity, commitment. Beyond the loud commercial calls of the auctioneer, the quiet concluding voice accepts the cost of experience and the human obligation to preserve the spirit of what has been. In this poem, as in many of the poems in this section, the sound and sense of the poetic voice overcomes the painful fact of loss, and the legacy remains.

In Cottonwood Township

Saturday night in Cottonwood Township:
milkweed fluff floats the moted dusk.
I pull a loose thread from my jeans
and the back pocket falls off.
This is the way of the township,
a loosening, then a loss.

A raveling thread of geese glides Cottonwood Township.
The river, like a sign on a beckoning inn,
blinks on and off.   Sunday
a daughter leaves for the city.
This is the way of the township,
a loosening, then a loss.

I gather milkweed pods, empty as cradles.
Painted, they glue into bright, brittle angels.
As I torch the ditch,
other pods snap, then vanish.
This is the way
of the township—a loosening,
then a loss.

Shirley Buettner

Telling Childhood

The kids glisten at the new bright mall
in his hometown. They do not care

for his old buried field
compressed beneath this parking lot

or how one spring the gypsies came,
garbled in costumes, language bright

as coins, to set up camp. Instead
they wide-eye all the marvels later

they'll relate: the elegant lights
for sparkling miles, trees inside of glass,

the twenty feet of waterfall
down artificial rock. He hears them tell

their children, who then shrug, entering
the abandoned lot at dusk, some smoky

campfires glowing in rubble,
music from a dozen patchy tents.

Robert King

Dakota Town

The elevator stands watchman,
its windows claimed
by the stones hurled by
boys who have left.
Now there are tires moaning
over the highway bringing
wind gusts past the last gas pump
where an old man in overalls watches
headlights and taillights
all day.

The streets are just Dakota summer dust
where the rain sinks untouched
to the sewers that have stopped their
hissings through the pipes,
and the out-houses are filled to the brim.

A farmer has jerked his country school
from its roots among the uncut weeds
and his haystack mover has taken it
to his home outside the town.
The church, the bar,
the hardware store and the lumberyard
have been claimed
for fences and windbreaks.

The graveyard lies at the edge
of a cornfield by the edge of town,
along the highway ditch,
the tombstones among sunflowers nodding
at the moaning tires going by.

Doug Cockrell

Roundhouse Ruins; Plattsmouth

The track has been ripped up,
the ties that held up tons
of steel and coal are dust.
Virginia creeper spikes
the brick walls, and the bricks
return to clay in a slow fire
of sun, a mold of air.

Here is where order ruled,
where one rich man's wish
sparked along thin wire
to twist the foreman's wrench,
to knock workers and boxcars
on or off the rails.

Out of these Romanesque doors
where they greased locomotives
to haul the hopes of a people
up the hump of depression
and war, down the easy hill
of better times, sunlight
pulls its heavy load of day.

S. C. Hahn

Dane Church Standing Empty Outside Red Cloud

The sky sends no missionaries.
Cold has snapped the summer drone
of insects,
heaven leans full on the treeless land
turning over and over
to the further rim of sky.

Prairie easily undoes the mind,
will not be counted
—unlike stars, whose pinwheel
    systems collapse on charts—
the prairie is not gathered into forms
the mind can cling to,
but falls away
like havens in dreams
the dreamer can never reach.

This church has closed around its time
like a memory,
although one of its windows
reflects the newly rocked road,
and above it,
the small gravestones fixed like stars.

Once this church was sturdy as a language,
and here, where silence comes
suddenly close
like the night voices of sleep,
the silence was pushed back
by curving furrows of sound,
in harmonies worked smooth as tools,
in hymns telling
of simple ascendencies
whitened to love
in distant stars.

Kris Vervaecke

In the Center of It

Eleven years
this farm has lived alone
has settled so far
into the soft dirt of neglect
even its memory has
grown weeds

Now a junked car raises its
family of skunk in the driveway

The bunkhouse where Indian Pete lived
has spit out all its windows
and with long, wooden breath
sucks in sparrows from the trees

The granary sits in its nest of firewood
like a great brown bird moulting

I have been to the house again
have read all the old copies of
the Post and Look
and watched a child grow tall
on the faded wall of a bedroom
his lines of age penciled in
among the rest

But here in the feedyard
there is nothing of that, no marks
to measure the passing of years and
only the wild eyes of the barn cats
seem to grow

The hog shed offers only
a dull red door pulled off
by the wind   It lies chipped
and frozen into the mud
held firm as a lost soul

I want to open it, to see the
tangle of pink bodies squealing
into the flesh of their Mother,

to feel the wet heat of milk on
November skin

Just once more I need to lie
in the afterbirth of that life

But the door clings heavily to Earth
and even
if my Father were alive
he could not help me lift it

Kevin Woster

Deserted Farm

Where the barn stood
the empty milking stalls rise up
like the skeleton of an ancient sea beast,
exiled forever on shores of prairie.

Decaying timber moans softly in twilight:
the house collapses like a broken prayer.
Tomorrow the heavy lilac blossoms will open,
higher than the roofbeams, reeling in wind.

Mark Vinz

Grandfather

Driving the team, he came up over
the hill and looked down. In the white bowl
of the snow-covered valley, his house
was aflame like a wick, drawing up
into itself all that he'd worked for.

Once, forty years later, we passed.
It was October. The cellar
was filled by a flame of young trees.
I got out, but he sat in the back
and stared straight ahead, this old, old man,
still tight on the reins of his years.

Ted Kooser

Valley of the Kaw

They lived here once, in this valley
where the moon hangs in the river
like the pocket watch of a president,
where smoke from a factory
festers like smallpox.

A warrior night hawk
shrieks out his last circle
and drops back into dark.

River, trees, and speechless ground—
they called themselves
the Children of the Wind.
Who will call our names
when we are gone?

Mark Vinz

Pioneer Cemetery

Field corner. Stones
they beat names
into with a fist. Wrenched
wire tight as love
pulling against fear
for a last fence.

Hand-planted trees.
Thin afterthought,
like singing to the dead.

Plows now cut
the dead corner short
to miss the trees.
Smooth stones.
A scrawl of wire,
their signature, a twist
of broken sentence
tangled in the grass.

Robert King

After School

After school
Ackerman's drugstore
smells faintly of medicine
and vanilla and dubblebubble
gum.
You buy rootbeer barrels
I stuff my jacksbag with long black licorice
twisted like snakes
like the snake Cleopatra
put against her skin.
We are spending five cents.

continued...

On the shaded afternoon steps
of Lowell School library
we play jacks
and wait for Martin Neilson
to shine past on his Elgin
bicycle.

The metal jacks say "chink"
on the smooth cement.
We throw them
and scoop them in.   We do
ups-and-downs
and lefts   and eggs-
in-the-basket.

When Martin Neilson
rides by with his newspapers
we stare hard at each other   we let
his spell freeze us
forever   spilling out stars
on the library steps.

On a dare   you raise your hand
to him   but Martin Neilson
(better-looking, even, than Dick Powell!)
doesn't see   grows smaller
and smaller   on his bicycle
riding out to the end of Maple
Avenue   to the beach
to his dry death   on the beach
at Anzio.

Barbara Esbensen

At the Vietnam Memorial

We look for names.
In the yellow pages of the dead
We thumb through.
Drizzle, cold, a numb day.

I do not find my names,
the men who disappeared
from my life.
This means they are still out there,
ricochetting through their days,
married, fathers,
gone to jobs,
to padded bars at night.
I check two times to make sure.

You find your name,
someone from high school,
and do not tell me more.
Lover? The tallest center
on the basketball team?
Look how he still stampedes
down the court, his eyes
permanent in the glare of light.
The floor-boards are slick, shiny.
And the ball released right now
from the grace of his body
goes up, over, and drops
like a severed head through the hoop.

We move down the marble gravestones.
So many, we cannot count,
we cannot help but see
our own bodies reflected,
pushed back at us darkly,
our faces tattooed with the
names of the dead.

Cary Waterman

Last Summer and the One Before

Father holds the melon
out from his buckle
as if a green container
about to christen the bow
of a new world. When the fruit
strikes the ground
I hear the meaning of broken.
With our hands
we scoop the heart crimson and sweet
into our mouths.
I spit a black seed
into a yellowing of yardlight,
turn to see a full moon
rising above the wheatfield
like the start of a new life.

*   *   *

Who knows why the tractor
slipped out of gear,
why its owner didn't look up
from his work at the sicklebar
sooner. I go to the funeral in a shirt
so stiff at the neck I am lost to say
who sat behind me.
Not even the fan overhead
can whirl away the heat
previewing hades, and Rock of Ages
drags like a four-bottom plow
choked time and again
with stubble. Heavens to Betsy, uncle says,
don't you know hardly
anything at all? Life is the learning of
which is which, the fixed law
or the sliding rule,
meaning, I guess, that because
I drink the last full dipper
I must take the bucket alone to be replenished
back to the deepening well.

William Kloefkorn

Could You Have Blinked and Not Seen It and Been Saved?

Six years old, I stared unblinking
at a black barrel leaned
against the wall you slumped against.
Death's blank stare had
pulled you past gravity.
Days later, still as your blood
pooled black on the floor,
I saw you again,
the black dot in the corner of your right eye
proof you wouldn't wake from this sleep.
Forty years beyond your coffin
you and I remain motionless forever
in a black hole of the mind,
two photographs
that swallowed our innocence.

Children of other ages do it again and
again, go in wars and crashes,
take themselves in numbers
those left try to understand,
to understand that
action simple and almost
motionless as a forefinger
curled around time's trigger
frames life surely
as a shot in an album.

Larry Holland

The Dream Collector

She sleeps with the net
beside her.
No dream escapes.
Waking
she sorts them by color
by country of origin.

The large butterfly
of her childhood
fills the north wall.

She mends
the torn silk wings
of her lovers
mounts them
under glass.

In a velvet case
her own death shimmers
gives off a faint
perfume.

Ruth Roston

Neighbor in May

my neighbor is hammering
and mending his house
he fixes in almost a frenzy
by night he dreams of his wife
dead nearly a year now
he dreams of nailing and healing
he dreams of repairing the damage

Michael Dennis Browne

Babicka's Funeral

Her children, remembering her for pastries
and parades, have covered her casket with sprays
of roses, unbecoming her, cherubic old lover
of marigolds she recycled year after year,
squeezing seeds like black slivers from frosty pods,
covering them with dirt in her yard too small
for roses, too humble for any other flower.

"She was never too tired to take us," they recall,
gathered around her casket. "How she loved clowns,
all powdered and costumed, as they marched
down the street." Her pastries, powdery too,
covered with sugar and icing, fillings of fruit,
black specks of poppyseed, offered company
beating marigold paths to the door.

"I want flour," she told us year after year,
whenever we asked. "Give me baking powder, sugar,
for Christmas," gifts she'd recycle in pastries
plumped into our mouths, warming holidays
for herself.

Now we circle around, while she, powdered,
costumed, lies covered with roses
draped in a spray. Outside the door, a black hearse
leads the parade lining up on the street.
She's wearing her favorite dress, a bright shade of marigold
clashing with roses, roses cascading as if they were naturally growing that way, as if she were riding a float
to the grave.

                                      Lorraine Duggin

Inheritance

I.

In the house are all her years
Buttons, string, linen dishtowels
Ironed, starched, folded
In drawers: fine wood,
Birds'-eye, hard rock maple
Which she oiled and rubbed.
I throw out her yellowed corsets
And white gloves.

Dust settles on windowsills.
I throw out the bottles of pills
For her heart, and small tins of rouge.
In the house is her King James,
Dried leaves,
Prayers clipped from newspapers
Pressed in its pages.
Somewhere, a photograph of a baby in a coffin.

The noon whistle blows.
I watch the minister as he walks home to lunch.
"Teach me, Lord,
To be gentle in all events, especially in disappointments,
Let me put myself aside."

II.

We like the kitchen, and put our own plants
On the sill. We hang a real slate board,
which we found in the cellar,
On the south wall.

This is where jelly bags hung in summer
With crab apple, buffalo berry;
where she laid a table out
In cloth and silver, filling each glass with water.
Her talk was of measuring, pouring, waiting.
This is where she made divinity and caramel
At Christmas.

III.

In June, 1917, men laid the sidewalk.
Children still skate on it, and learn to bicycle.

I keep her garden,
Worrying for the spent columbine and daisy
That sleep through the winter in beds of straw.
Their dreams are mine: the first leaves out,
Sheets that smell of earth and sky.

The rainbarrel stands
Full of dark water, in the dark.
It opens its mouth as if to speak.

Kathleen Norris

Grandfather Sonnenberg

He'd become the family myth.
They were guided by joy
which seeped easily up
through a dark ground of pain.
He had suffered through deaths
of his children and his woman.
The invisible needle teeth of cancer
had now and again nibbled his flesh,
and alone in his fields, his hand caught
in the crushing molars of his cornpicker,
he had beaten it off at the wrist
with a three-pound crescent wrench. O,
they say his smile was serene,
that his face glowed like a field of grain
touched   by an August sun.
They say that pain, for them,
has been lessened forever,
as if somehow filtered
through the ragged body
of their grandfather.

Joe Paddock

The Gift

I am ready now to admit
That I failed at everything
Except perhaps at once quick span
Of crisis, when I said yes
To my dying father and
To his only piece of acreage.
Gifts are not easy to accept,
Not when they nudge you to
The sudden wall of your stubbornness.
But at thirty I lay awake, alone,
Dreaming growth. I had failed
At everything, but when
I touched the land again
And heard my father's voice
I saw but one image:
Not the pondless pasture
Or the unpainted house
Or even the rock,
But a single seed.
I said, *Yes.*

William Kloefkorn

Pigeons of My Youth

They never give up,
those pigeons of my youth.
Look: under the bluff,
they nod, step quick,
picking up spilled corn
between the tracks.

When two box cars—
iron fists—
wham together
away they go

a fleet cloud rising
over the creosote steps,
over the hill street's
houses, up, up. . .

later, when the rusty
grains of noise
settle,
look again: they're
picking up spilled corn
between the tracks.

David Allan Evans

Our First Generation of Old Men

There were Kingsryder and McGraw
back then.
McGraw ran the coffee shop.
Kingsryder was an old man
who dressed each day in a black suit
and black, high-topped old man's shoes,
and carried a cane for the power that was in it.

>   Back then
>   it seemed that all of this had gone on forever,
>   but these prairies had only just been turned.
>   This was our first generation of old men,
>   violent as old bull buffalo on their knees,
>   bubbling their last blood.

Each day at three in the afternoon, Kingsryder,
entering the coffee shop, all bustle and self-importance
around some emptiness within, I suppose,

>   or maybe just that storm
>   of hellish fun,

Would whack his cane on the counter
for attention,
call for donuts and coffee,
begin his noisy complaint,   dead pan:
"McGraw, you got an old garbage pile 'round back
where you get these donuts?"
Then lifts his cup: "McGraw, whose radiator'd you
drain today?"

>   These two men over many years had never once
>   embraced.
>   Never once had thrown a friendly arm around
>   the other's shoulder.

>   Perhaps, even, never once shaken hands.

And McGraw, over the years, always irritated,
would only say, "Kingsryder, one of these days
I'm gonna shoot you!"

And *whack!* goes the cane across a counter that
not twenty years back had been an oak
on the Darwin Prairie.
"Draw your weapon, McGraw! Play your hand!"

And so McGraw sent away somewhere
for a box of blanks
for his old hog-leg revolver,
and comes the day—there's a half dozen coffee soaks
    there—
when Kingsryder asks:
"McGraw, you got a deal with old Moon Beckstrand
what cleans the streets?"
And McGraw says, deadly between his teeth:

"Kingsryder, I've told you!"
Then he reaches slow under the counter,
comes up with his revolver,
and the place is so still
that you can hear
a crow cawing for something lost
way off at the edge of town.
Kingsryder's cane wavers. Not a snake-tongue
flicker,
but a waver,   like the antenna
of a confused insect.

        How does an old Indian fighter die,
            when, in fact, he'd never really . . . ?

McGraw's face is cold.
KA-BAM! goes the piece.
Kingsryder's eyes show white in a faint,
and he slides from his stool to the floor,
and the six coffee-drinkers pass through the door
        like whippets,
shouting:

"McGRAW SHOT KINGSRYDER!
    McGRAW SHOT KINGSRYDER!"

We laughed about it for years. It tuned up our lives,
and emptied Kingsryder of half his style.

continued. . .

Who's to say the fright didn't knock a bit from
    the tail end of Kingsryder's days?
Or who's to say Kingsryder's insults hadn't done
as much for McGraw.
They're both gone now.
They were our first generation of old men,
violent as old bull buffalo on their knees, bubbling
their last blood.

Joe Paddock

Frogs

From a story told by Delmar Debbaut

At that time there was still a pothole
over every hill, and the frogs in the fall
swarmed like maggots in the carcass of a
dead horse.
Sometimes, after the coming of the cars,
they had to get out the blade to scrape the slick
of crushed frogs off that road that circles
Stork Lake.

One sunny Saturday afternoon in late September,
more than forty years back now,
down around the bay,
about fifteen town kids began to herd frogs
up from the water's edge where they lay
dozing in the sun by the thousands,
big heavy leopard frogs that would stretch
nine, ten inches from nose to toe claw.

They herded them slowly
up over Anderson's pasture hill.
You would've thought it was wind through grass
sweeping ahead of them.
Herded them up onto the road into town,
herded them with real care, losing a few here
    and there,

but maintaining the mass
(some guessed five thousand, some ten),
and at the corner of Sixth,
they turned them, losing maybe forty dozen
which bounced on over Hershey's lawn,
confusing the beJesus out of their old Basset
        hound, Monty,
who, after sniffing and poking with his paw,
sat down and howled at a thin silver sliver
        of day moon
in the sky.

Old Mrs. Angier said she first heard a sound
like five thousand hands patting meat,
and when she looked up the street, she saw
these kids, serious and quiet, with a grey-brown
        wave,
like swamp water to their knees,
rolling along in front of them.

Mrs. Angier said, "Now, you never heard a word
from a single one of those kids.
They were silent and strange with that haze of a wave
rolling along in front of them.
Just that patting sound
times five thousand.
I tell you, it made goose flesh roll
up my back and arms!"

The boys claimed later that they had no plan,
but, when they came alongside "Horse" Nelson's
Fixit Quick Garage—which contained
maybe a half dozen broken-down cars
and "Horse" and Allen, his son, and "Windy"
        Jeffers—
one kid barked: "Bring 'em on in!"
and they turned that herd of frogs on a dime
(they were herding easy by that time),
and ran them through the entranceway.
Young Jim Hedeen grabbed the handle
of the sliding door and rolled her shut,
and those kids vanished like fifteen rabbits
into whatever weed patch they could find.

continued. . .

Well, hell, you can imagine.
"Windy" was on his back working upward on a
    spring
when those slimy devils started sliding all
    over him.
They say he most-near tipped that Model A
    on its side
getting out of there. And "Horse,"
who was no doubt nearly through his daily pint
of peach brandy, dropped a cam shaft
on Allen's toe and ran and hid in the can,
and Allen, who'd been mean and noisy
from his first squawk on, began hopping
    one-footed
amidst that froth of frogs. (And you *know*
how they have a way of climbing
up the inside of your pants, all wet
and with those scratchy little claws!)
Allen, slam-banging whatever came to hand,
tipped a couple cars from jacks, and screamed:
"I'M GONNA GET KEVIN KLIMSTRA FOR THIS!"

Forty-three years have passed,
but those frogs have never quit rolling
from the tongues of people around town.
It's one of those stories you learn early
and carry with you, and measure
the taste of life by
till the day you die.

Joe Paddock

Ritual

After
Christmas dinner
we talk as we always do
over wine goblets and coffee cups.
The young roll their eyes and seek escape
as they always do, leaving in pairs and packs,
having heard too many Uncle Lawrence stories,
recalling Grandpa's second bride only as a testy old woman
with no eyebrows. We remain, retelling our tales,
and letting the circle widen to include the dead.
The young imagine their lives as straight lines.
One day they will round a corner and find
themselves circling back, telling stories
after Christmas dinner,
letting the circle widen
to include
us.

Nancy Veglahn

My Granddaughter, Age 3, Tells Me the Story of the Wizard of Oz

There is a brain, she says,
right here, she says,
pointing to the front of her head,
but the Scarecrow
doesn't have one yet,
not until the end of the story.

And there is a heart, she says,
right here, she says,
pushing an index finger
hard against her chest,
but the Tin Man
will not have it
until the end of the story.

And there is courage, she says,
right here, she says,
pushing a fist against her stomach,
but the Lion will not have it
unless I tell the story.
Shall I tell the story?

Yes, I say, tell the story,
all of it, from beginning to end.

And I am swept up with Dorothy and Toto
up and away to a place
far removed from myself,
to the truth all over again
that nothing is true until told,
not the brain, not the heart, not courage,

not even the witch, who is the last to go,
the teller now in absolute control,
her eye the eye of all storms set straight

at the end of the story.

William Kloefkorn

Estate Sale

the furniture of her life
spread over the yard for strangers
eyes   and fingers
feel for something solid
some thread
from the whole cloth
of the past

polished brass bed
the heavy oak table and buffet
her best china
Red Wing crocks   boxes
of clouded zinc-capped Mason jars

all for sale
all drowning
in the quick litany
of the auctioneer:

"What'll ya give me?"

he picks through sheets and towels
with crocheted edges
grabs up an armload of quilt:

"What do I hear? A dollar?
C'mon, do I hear two?"

for more than a hundred hours of work

I can't resist
bid ten dollars to take home
the pieces of a life   bound together
a patchwork
of tiny-flowered baby clothes
splashy apron paisleys
tired blue stripes of a husband's pajamas

a pattern of her own   created
with patience
of the slow silent mending

continued . . .

of wounds

women's work
made to be used   worn out
to keep us warm

because my mother   and my grandmother
did not make quilts
I'll sleep tonight
beneath the stitches of a stranger
who sleeps
beneath the ground
and the thread   unbroken
passes on to me

Nancy Paddock

Each to Each

One of the loneliest and most desolate statements in literature is this one in T. S. Eliot's "The Love Song of J. Alfred Prufrock":

> *I should have been a pair of ragged claws*
> *Scuttling across the floors of silent seas.*

Prufrock feels out of touch, unloved, unrecognized. He has romantic impulses, hearing mermaids singing "each to each," but he can't hope that they will sing to him, or that anyone will. He thinks that he might as well be isolated not only in the distance which is ocean but *beneath* that uninterrrupted expanse. He doesn't even suggest that he should have been a crab, a whole thing with at least a generic identity, but simply the claws, the almost purely mechanical parts of the creature. And even those parts should be "ragged." Prufrock is tragically unable to make connections or have relationships, and so he feels valueless.

In dramatic contrast, there is this prose poem by contemporary writer N. Scott Momaday which summarizes traditional Native American relationships with all of creation:

> *You see, I am alive.*
> *You see, I stand in good relation to the earth.*
> *You see, I stand in good relation to the gods.*
> *You see, I stand in good relation to all that is beautiful.*
> *You see, I am alive, I am alive.*

The speaker of these celebratory words feels totally connected to everything material and spiritual, and *because* of those feelings, he is fully and intensely "alive."

This complicated and difficult matter of relationships, so often a theme in literature, is explored from a variety of perspectives in this section. In the first selection, "In the Fresh Air," one of the most common symbols of relationship, the wedding, is presented in a very ominous way. In the first stanza, there is "hissing" rather than the traditional kissing, and at the end of the poem the couple's eyes are "blank," although eyes are usually the most expressive features and should be especially expressive at a time like this. In the poem that follows, "One September Afternoon," there are also two people who seem more comfortable with objects than with each other.

In the next selection, "The Wide Receiver," the woman wants to talk to her husband about their relationship and their future, but he is preoccupied by the past and by his failing football career. And in "The Swiss Chalet Barometer" and "An Old Photograph," there are horrifying pictures of couples living separately together, alienated from each other through time and experience. The works which follow those,

"Divorce Court," "The Weeping Willow," and "Phoning My Son Long Distance," explore the consequences of making alienation official through legal process.

Then there are selections about the difficulty of establishing and maintaining good family relationships. At the end of "Sunday Afternoon Drive Near the Cliffs Outside of Town," the family seems to have only terror in common. In "Keeping the Horses," an alcoholic father has left his son alone, and the boy is divided between the possibility of his father's return and his impulse to run wild like the horses and be solitary and free. "Photo of Women Plowing" is a very grim portrayal of estranged women "more bitter before son or husband" than before their expressionless employer, and in "Uncle Adler," alienation within the family is apparently so great that greed is the only motivation.

In the story which follows, "Not Much Unsettled or Disturbed," there are also family difficulties, grief and guilt and regret in response to the father's death, but added to those there is hope. At the end, the narrator is thinking about the possibility of the beginning of love. Similarly, in the poem that follows, "The Mexican Girl," the speaker fantasizes about his chances of a romantic relationship, and the woman described in "Symptoms," the poem after that, lives on the romances she imagines.

But "reaching out" to make contact is difficult, as demonstrated by the next cluster of poems, which focus on our primary means of physical touch, our hands. In "Old Soldiers' Home" and "Old Men's Hands In Their Laps," once active hands are sadly idle, resting in laps. But in the poems entitled "Hands," touching is dominant, as hands move and work and connect past and present, establishing relationships between the old and the young. In those poems and in "The Auction," hands are healing and affirmative.

"The Junkman," the next work in the section, suggests that even extreme alienation can be overcome through common experience, and the poem after that, "Christmas Eve," is an emotional tribute to the bond which can develop in time. In that poem, hands are again symbols of what can be shared.

Then there are works about the relationship we call "community." In "July," even though individuals are alienated from each other in many ways, community is evoked through the ringing bells, as healing as rain at the end of the poem. And in "Nebraska," the townspeople are intricately interrelated in their small rural society.

At the end of this section, there are poems about relationships with the natural world, and about the larger consequences of those relationships. "Neighbor" dramatizes the distance between humans and nature, but it also reminds us of a very long co-existence. In

"Gathering," the dying aunt is the energetic center of a profusion of green life, and in the end the poet seems comforted by remembering her in those terms. In "A Love Letter," the speaker asks his love to come not only to him but to his natural environment—to participation with and celebration of natural things. Similarly, "Mulch" and "Composting" are companion poems about integration and natural process, reciprocal relationships with the physical world.

The concluding works in this section, "So This is Nebraska," "Silo Singing," "Wedding Song," and "Sunday Morning," are pure celebrations of what naturally is. "Sunday Morning," especially, is bright with light and promise. The lonely sound of the mourning dove is followed by images of love, family, and faith, to which even the solitary bird responds as the poem ends. Here, at least temporarily, is dramatic contrast to Eliot's ironically entitled "Love Song," and an echoing of the "good relations" in Momaday's incantory summary of what life should be.

In the Fresh Air

A wedding floated up along the sand
path between the hissing grasses, the man
leaning over in his tall hat and striped pants
to eye the trees, while the new wife walked
tall under her white parasol, her silk
elbow nestled in his back, and the lace
of the white bridesmaid behind like a fluffed
stork's feathers hissed among the leaves as she
smiled sailing the blossomy morning air.

I sat on a riverbank grinning
into a newspaper as they came on
with the moving clouds and boats and shadows;
I grinned because I glanced at their eyes
and saw they were blank, blued, and quite steady.

Antony Oldknow

One September Afternoon

Home from town
the two of them sit
looking over what they have bought
spread out on the kitchen table
like gifts to themselves.
She holds a card of buttons
against the new dress material
and asks if they match.
The hay is dry enough to rake,
but he watches her
empty the grocery bag.
He reads the label
on a grape jelly glass
and tries on
the new straw hat again.

Leo Dangel

The Swiss Chalet Barometer

for twenty years
they have not spoken
to one another

on sunny days
she shuffles across the threshhold
to water her window boxes
and he sulks inside
by the chimney

when the weather worsens
she sits in her dim kitchen
singing her song
to no one
while he stands raging
on the doorstep

so it is with one marriage
half-lives in a dark house

Shirley Buettner

The Wide Receiver

One.

When the ball comes sliding down a hillside of air and he connects with it, for a moment he feels light pulsing beneath the skin of his hands.

He's thinking about the feel of that light as he lines up near the sideline on this last play of the game. He's thinking how he loves to see that ball rise toward him, spiralling above the defensive linemen's outstretched arms. He's trying not to think of splintered elbows. The world's waiting to splinter your elbows, his father used to say. He's thinking how much depends on his own two hands.

Just catch the ball, his woman says, reminding him.

When he's wrapped up in the whole game with its strategies and fancy moves, its complex plays, its chalkline diagrams like piles of spiders on a chalkboard, he hears her voice saying something so simple it hurts: catch the ball.

His wife knows him, knows what he really needs. Come closer, she said last night as they sat alone on the living room carpet. It's a kind of love she's talking about when she says the shortest distance between two people is not a straight line, but an arc, and the only way it can travel is fingertip to fingertip.

He knows the feeling of weightlessness as he listens to the signals. It's fine. It's right for him. Apart from the huge, hunchbacked linemen, he has the freedom to stand upright, like the fittest of humans. His feet caress grass that seems never to have been walked upon.

Some nights when they sit at home on the carpeting, she reminds him that one day soon he'll have to give it up. It's enough recognition, enough fame. She says he should save himself from the awful staining bruises, the crippled limbs that await him. Save his legs so some day he can still run and catch a rubber football in the yard with a son.

But he tells her he's not in pain out there. Pain is what those

continued . . .

people in the stands feel when they watch him and yearn to be like him. It's their hunger. Their thirst as they eat handfuls of popcorn nervously. He catches the ball as much for them as he does for himself, and then he braces to get hit, the glass tubes of his legs hit hard but not shattering. He comes down on his elbows but does not let the ball—will not let it— jar loose. In that moment, there's no pain: he's one with the fans, and the sound of their screams is like the light from a flashbulb surrounding his skin.

.

Time, he thinks. You've always got to watch the clock in this game. They're always timing you: in the huddle, between plays. He squints toward the scoreboard and sees the silver blink of the numbers: falling, always falling.

The ball is snapped. His two hands. Two legs. Everything's in halves, quarters, in twos. He sprints eight yards toward the 40. He knows the score: fourth quarter, a few seconds to go in the game. He knows that the silent air which surrounds his body must be cut through by an angel of leather. Knows he must pull that angel softly to the center of his body, knows he must catch it or it will die. He fakes near the defender, then turns as the pass leaves his quarterback's hands. Bits of turf fly from his cleats like the trailings of a comet. For a moment it looks as if the pass is going straight up, an awkward bird fluttering from tree stumps. But the word is long, long.

Fingertip to fingertip.

Two.

Once, in grade school, he read about what Henry Ford did when his closest friend Thomas Edison was on his death bed. They agreed that when Edison was about to die, his last breath would be caught in a glass test tube.

He read the article several times, and never forgot it. He always thought about the wonder of such an idea. It was bizarre, but wasn't it an act of love and generosity, an attempt to catch and prolong his dead friend's final living moment and to preserve it in all its clarity for future generations? Perhaps, by agreeing to this, it was Edison who gave us his all, his final sigh of genius. Perhaps, years later, some newborn, taking in his first air, might be given the breath through an oxygen mask. What might that child become?

.

Before the big games, he sits in a chair at home and repeats, in his mind, a phrase every coach he's known has admitted to be true: No one can stop a perfect pass, no one can stop a perfect pass.

Sometimes she interrupts his thinking. Sometimes she calls the plays. She wants to talk about the two of them: their future, the seasons ahead. She says she's worried. It's all right, he tells her, don't get down. It's all right. And he knows that when he says this to her, he's really trying to convince himself.

You can't let yourself get down; you have to take chances, risks. You have to dive for the ones you know you can't reach, dive for them anyway. Even when you miss one, you learn. Sometimes he creates a catch—invents it out of nowhere on a ball badly underthrown or overthrown. Once, when he leaped into the blue to catch a high, impossible pass, for an instant he actually believed he could take flight. It was at that moment he thought he felt her hands around his legs, pulling him gently back down to the turf.

.

Fine print. Sometimes he can't read the fine print in the newspaper, and she notices him adjusting the paper away from his face. You'll be needing glasses soon, she says. No, he says. Just an eyelash. An eyelash in my eye.

.

He often remembers his early years, the way his face mask got in the way as a pass approached. In high school, at the first practice, he couldn't recognize his best buddies when they slid on their helmets. Without foreheads or chins they became Neanderthals, brutal and dangerous. He learned, those first weeks, to recognize his friends not by their faces, but by the markings on their helmets. Scuff marks: the hieroglyphics of pain.

Now he's accustomed to his helmet and mask, and the way they've saved his eyes from being gouged by rusty cleats. Lately he's thinking he can see better with his helmet on than with it off. He mentioned that to her once at dinner. No, she just said. No.

.

It will be luck. A large part of making a reception is luck. The

continued ...

catch depends on unexpected elements: a slip of the quarterback's index finger, a sudden gust of wind, a stumble of defender. If it's right, though, it will be the accident of perfection.

On certain plays, when the ball is thrown right to him, chest high, a strange thought sometimes occurs to him: drop it. Too easy. Drop it.

Three.

More and more lately they've been referring to him as a veteran. The great veteran, they call him. He's got the lockerful of records, he's got the following. A veteran is a man with experience, they say, but he knows the real meaning of the word: it's a man who's teetering on an edge, a man whose muscles are turning to putty, a man who has trouble hearing the signals when he lines up, a man who might be taking in his last few breaths.

For a time, high school seemed so close, but now it has pulled quickly away from him. But he still sleeps on it some nights, like a field of soft grass and pompons. Then that old dream cuts in front of him: the pass he got his hands on in the high school championship. Thirty seconds left in the game. His hands were too anxious, too stiff. The bobbled ball spun end over end in front of his face, and a defender clamped his arms to his sides and the ball fell slowly, harmlessly onto the grass. His father's face in the stands was like a hole in a broken window. He could almost hear his father's voice: they're waiting, the world's waiting. At the end of the dream, he hears the ball at his feet, hissing like a bad tire losing air.

They say you must get tired of the repetition—the announcers say it, the sports writers. The fans agree. They say you must get tired of lining up at scrimmage, or the quick burst out to the flat, tired of years of tacklers knocking your body over like a stack of dominoes. The joints start to soften, the hinges give, and tiny fires begin in ankle and knee. Some days coordination seems to be evaporating from you like sweat. And when you reach to catch the ball, a helmet jars it loose from the webs of your fingers. Then there's the jog back to huddle, the empty hands placed on knees. They say you must get tired. And they tire of you.

But there's something inside him, some center of brightness that won't let him stop sprinting his fastest, even though he knows the play will be miles from him. What is it? That's what she wants to know when they talk. What is it that makes him keep going, season after season, when he should be giving it up? Why does he push himself too far, like a man wavering near the edge of a stadium roof? He shakes his head; he can't answer. Because all his life he couldn't shape his lips around an answer, he shaped his hands around an oval football.

These two hands, he thinks. They answer for him. It's all worth it when the quarterback sends a ball sailing across the ocean of air toward him and his hands fasten to leather as if they're in love with it.

Then he thinks of the way the ball's been dropping lately, rocking awkwardly back and forth on the turf for a moment.

What about it? she asks. What about the two of us?

Leather silence. Leather silence.

He's panting as he takes long strides toward the goal post. He watches the ball approaching, watches every spin of its seams. Eyes. Your eyes must be able to see a scratch on a phonograph record from across a room. He remembers talking to her last night about repainting the kitchen. A change, she said. A fresh coat of paint to make the woodwork, the walls all look new. But what color? What color. They couldn't decide, and began arguing about it. He wanted blue, blue like the color of distant sky, and she wanted unobtrusive white. Just plain antique white. Cleaner, she said, simpler. Not clean, he said—indistinct, ordinary. Pure, she said. Paint that's new will stay new at least a year. That's not long enough, he said. My father always said paint a wall dark and you'll hide the imperfections. Your father, your father she said. Your father's dead.

He pressed his face against the darkened kitchen window, his breath steaming the glass. Then she apologized, and leaned close to his ear and whispered something that terrified him, though it shouldn't have. When are we going to have a baby? she asked.

Decisions. Decisions are never easy. From the line of scrimmage, there always seem to be gaping holes in the defense, holes that quickly close like snares once you set foot inside them.

Let's talk about planning, she told him later. He shrugged.

Open the calendar, she said. Look at it. This is winter. Winter. Don't you know what season you're in?

Of course, he told her. Of course I do.

continued . . .

That evening he walked around the house with his shoes untied. He stooped to tie them, lost his balance in the middle of the living room. His fingers sunk deep into the carpet. He sat and squinted at the gray TV screen. He pulled the pop top on a can of beer. The vacuum inside it sighed.

Four.

Every moment the last moment. A few seconds left in the game, and as the ball begins to descend, the wide receiver knows this play will mean everything.

His best fake didn't even catch the defender off balance— the man's rich rookie blood makes his whole body liquid. They're step for step toward the end zone, the chalk lines blinking beneath them like dusty white years. The crowd's roar is miles away now, and filled with static like an old record. Then all sound fades except for the hush of air through the two men's lips.

He thinks how this defender is second skin, thinks how his eyes are baby blue and scared. Got to shake him.

A child, she says, a child. Someone to live beyond us.

After fifty yards of flight, the ball's a seamless, perfect spiral, with a small window of light glistening on its top. It's the arc, the rise and the fall of it, that hypnotizes him.

Over my head, he thinks, too high to reach. His answer is a leap, that motion smooth as love: the right snap of knee, the unity of muscle and bone. Up, it takes him, above the shoulders of the defender, up. And he seems to keep rising: he holds his breath, as if he could push his forehead through the blue tissue of sky. Fingertip to fingertip.

And from this height he exhales a breath: a clear, memorable breath that keeps rising beyond him into the open palm of the sky.

Bill Meissner

An Old Photograph

This old couple, Nils and Lydia,
were married for seventy years.
Here they are sixty years old
and already like brother
and sister—small, lustreless eyes,
large ears, the same serious line
to the mouths. After those years
spent together, sharing
the weather of sex, the sour milk
of lost children, barns burning,
grasshoppers, fevers and silence,
they were beginning to share
their hard looks. How far apart
they sit; not touching at shoulder
or knee, hands clasped in their laps
as if under each pair was a key
to a trunk hidden somewhere,
full of those lessons one keeps
to himself.
          They had probably risen
at daybreak, and dressed
by the stove, Lydia wearing
black wool with a collar of lace,
Nils his worn suit. They had driven
to town in the wagon and climbed
to the studio only to make
this stern statement, now veined
like a leaf, that though they looked
just alike they were separate people,
with separate wishes already
gone stale, a good two feet of space
between them, thirty years to go.

Ted Kooser

Divorce Court

We had to stand for the judge. Firing squads
command the same respect. Rapid fingers
took down everything that passed for words.
Our tables were islands, our lawyers malingering
sharks, to whom we fed each other. Stripped
to bone, we testified. Our children's names
flew all around like birds who would escape,
brightly colored. Her crippled mother came
across three states to tell the court the organ
was her daughter's. I had to read aloud
from my checkbook, bedtime stories for bad kids.
and once a beautiful blindfolded woman
wandered in by mistake but was soon turned
out. No one could smoke, though I burned, I burned.

Philip Dacey

The Weeping Willow

The boy sat staring out the window, his eyes set straight ahead, the scene wavy. It was theirs, this house, this yard. What right had these strangers—the man and the woman, their whining daughter, and the grinning real estate agent—to walk on the grass they had reseeded that spring, to lean on their fence as casually and intimately as if it had been their own? The right allowed by the FOR SALE sign on the front lawn, the grownups would answer. But weren't there other rights that counted too? Why couldn't they understand? His father, who had built him the tree house in their sprawling maple, and the slat steps up to it, he should understand. And his mother, who just last year had labored with him over the planting of the weeping willow he had wanted to watch grow up to the size of the one in his grandfather's yard—had she forgotten how to understand? But then, this was the second time they had betrayed him.

The first time had been, not the divorce itself, for he had accepted that, somehow, at the time. Besides, there had been some compensations. Before the divorce, his parents had been loving strangers to him. His father chucked him under the chin and brought him delightful surprises. His mother kept the cookie jar full and tucked him in at night, after a story. Then, in the aftermath of the divorce, they had come to know one another, he and his father, he and his mother. He and his father went camping together, just the two of them. They discovered the same colors in the sunsets and the same shapes in the clouds. He and his mother read together the C.S. Lewis *Chronicles of Narnia* and Antoine St. Exupery's *The Little Prince*, and they talked together, in the long quiet evenings, about what they found in the books, and in life. They talked about Aslan, that gentle lion, about his goodness and his courage, and about that little prince, with his love for a rose, which he nurtured without consideration of dangers or sacrifices. And it was good, then. At that time, he felt no betrayal.

Only later, when his father would often change their together plans for others. When his mother would not be in the kitchen when he came home from school, but typing in an office downtown, when the ghost of her absence loomed so large it formed a lump in his throat, and he could not swallow the cookies and milk, his after-school snack. When he saw families together at the park or in the grocery store, or when his friends talked about their family vacations to Disneyland or Yellowstone. When it seemed to rain every day, even though the ground was always dry.

continued . . .

One night at the dinner table the words poured out before he even knew they were on his mind. "You could bring him back home if you wanted to!" He had watched her face move all over and then collapse, like a deflated rubber ball. He had to be triumphant at her suffering, because of his own.

After that, the boy's father came more often to the house, for Sunday dinners, after which he and the boy's mother would sit together on the love seat on the porch, talking long and pensively, or in the evenings, when the two of them would take long drives together in his father's LTD Country Squire Wagon, lingering to talk on a while before his mother would come into the house. It would be all right. He was certain it would be all right. Then, on one of those nights, a night his mother had lingered particuarly long in the car, she asked the boy to sit with her on the porch, in the faintly autumn air. She was sorry, she told him. He must understand that he could not hope for his father to come back home.

He understood only that he had counted on her, and she had let him down. Both of them had let him down. So, often, on long nights he could not sleep, he would, in the recreation room downstairs, with the sound turned low, run the movies from the days he remembered most fondly, the days of birthday parties and homemade ice cream, of board games on winter Sunday afternoons and Christmas mornings around the packaged tree. If he couldn't have those days back, couldn't they at least let him keep their setting a while longer? They could if they wanted to, he was certain. He wondered which one of them was selling him out, along with the house. How do you know which to believe in, when you need to believe in both of them. Maybe you stop believing in either of them. That might be safest. Believe in no one and re-run the years you could believe in. He especially liked to run the birthday scenes backward, to watch the candles puff on instead of out.

Now, from his chair, he watched until the strangers left in the agent's bronze Cadillac. Then he went out to the yard and stared at the sign, his enemy. He stared long and hard, and suddenly, the sign was in his hands, uprooted. He was not quite sure how it had happened, but there it was, and he had to decide what to do about it. Of course he could always put it back. He did not put it back. He held it close against his body and sidled around the corner of the house, along the length of the north side, and then he took a series of running leaps across the back yard to the maple tree. He climbed the slat ladder up to the tree house, the sign still clutched against him. It would not fit through the trap door, so he had to chance an awkward reach to push it over the edge onto the floor. Then he climbed in himself. He pulled a limp plastic bag out of a wedge between two branches and opened it—a marking pen, a tangle of rubber bands, two Band Aids, a hammer and screwdriver, an assortment of nails and screws, and a package of raisins. He wasn't hungry, though. With the marking pen, he amended the sign to read NOT FOR SALE. He nailed it to the rail of the tree house and settled down not to think. But the thoughts pounded in, like the nails he had pounded into the sign.

If he could have been nine again, or even ten, he might have thought with comfort of the lion Aslan, or he might have borrowed the tears the small prince shed for his beloved rose. But from ten to eleven, he had aged a span longer than a year. Now the rescuing roar of Aslan seemed very far distant, and it no longer seemed permissible to cry. He could not even, any longer, see the light he had identified as the plant of the little prince glowing in the sky, although it was nearly dusk.

A gust of wind came up, suddenly, and the leaves whirred, like the movie frames. The figures in the movies blurred away. They had all deserted him. Every last one of them. Below, to the left, across a stretch of lawn, the willow wept.

Geraldine A.J. Sanford

Phoning My Son Long Distance

Surely I know that
my voice has grown small in his house,
drawn thin by the wire,
a fly's whine in the clutter of breakfast,
a thin line of ants
winding out of a crack in the past
toward the sweet, impossible cup of his ear.

In the background, my former wife is whispering.
I clutch at the phone like a hand held down.
It grows more difficult for me
to crawl into the hot cardboard fort of his love
simply by phoning on Sundays.

Ted Kooser

Sunday Afternoon Drive Near the Cliffs Outside of Town

All we kids did was ask dad to drive off the road
a little closer to the cliff.
He cracked the ignition switch
off, let our '52 Rambler roll
gradually toward the edge
until we saw nothing but raw air
outside the windshield.
Mom squeezed his elbow
but his eyes pinched into BBs, his knuckles
clenched the wheel as though he loved
or hated it.
He eased his foot off
the wheezing brake. We rocked
nearer, gravel stuttering under tires.
He kept us there,
the dashboard clock dropping hard seconds
into the front seat,
our screams filling the back seat
like weights.
But he wouldn't
back up, as if he wanted the whole family
to fly, or die.
He laughed when he finally steered
us toward the city limits,
but all we kept seeing
were those monstrous brown boulders
far below us
looking like too many wrecked houses.

Bill Meissner

Keeping the Horses

The boy had been alone for fifteen days
before the thought occurred to him: this time
maybe the old man wasn't coming back
at all. It was just him and the horses,
feeding their way around the tether-stakes
in a good bit of meadow by the road,
the boy sleeping out with them at night
upon the ground (the nights not yet grown cold),
by daylight watching over them until
he half suspected when he talked to them
they were about to answer —those great eyes,
the telltale shivers in the flank and haunch.
Even the horses had been feeling it,
the small uneasiness that moved inside him.
He brushed them down, went to fetch water
up from the creek a hundred yards away;
hauling it back, he heard the water sway
and lap against the bucket at his side.
A car went by from the farm down the road.
He waved, and the driver waved, and the dust
swept out and made a tunnel in the air —
a tunnel that would suddenly collapse.
And he thought of his mother through the years
trying to glimpse, like that, his father's quick,
authoritative passage through their lives.
He would be drinking now, talking about his plans
with someone he hardly knew in some dark bar,
the truck and van parked outside, the dust
of this same road on top of other dust
from all the roads they'd driven down that year,
following the circuit of the county fairs
with a ramshackle carnival, the horses
sometimes performing in a lot out back
and sometimes to a grandstand audience.
Near towns down those back roads, more and more of late,
they'd pull off onto the grassy shoulder
by a gate that led into a pasture,
backing the animals down the splintered ramp,
his father fashioning a long rope halter

continued . . .

to lead one horse around with at a time
and give the local kids a ride. It cost
two bits some days, on other days a dime,
the difference being what the old man lacked
by way of change to jangle in his jeans.
It always went for drink —always for that.
There was never any money for the boy;
the old man never thought that anyone
had needs except himself. And they were poor,
God, but they were poor! Many a time
they'd lifted out the seat up in the cab,
just to scrounge around for coins: in fun
they called it "going to the bank." (He thought
of the old man, frantic for money now,
lying across the pitted running-board,
his long legs out at angles in the street
like toppled stilts beside the worn-out seat,
hoping to pick up on the littered floor
a beer or two in change . . .)

                              The sun had dipped
into the lower branches of the cottonwoods
down by the creek. Every day now that moment came
a little sooner, and the boy saw how
the grass went deep and almost wet with light
at that lower angle. He walked back down
toward the stand of trees for some kindling wood.
One thing that you could say for the old man:
there was always plenty of food in cans
for cooking over a fire; as for talk,
they'd never come close to running out of that.
Still, with him gone, he didn't miss the talk.
It was good to have the outdoors to himself,
or the feeling of that, the horses there
stirring and nickering, snuffling in the dark
beyond the fire, the stars darting their glints
far back down to him from a wet black sky.
The first few days it seemed to him as if
the old man were still around; but lately
he'd noticed he'd begun to let things go,
begun to grow wild along with the horses.
There were times he wished he could run like them,
the ground reverberating under him,
nothing between him and the open sky

but his shadow floating out over the grass . . .

He rummaged in the canvas knapsack bottom
for the opener, For supper he'd have beans,
cooked in a shallow pan until the bubbles
snapped in the juice like lava on the run —
nothing better, sopped with a hunk of bread.
He thought he'd move the tether-stakes tonight;
then maybe afterwards he'd leave the fire
and walk down by the bridge to listen
to the water gurgling in its glimmering banks.
One of these nights the old man would be back,
and more and more his thoughts were fixed on that.
For several days he'd had a kind of dream
shaping inside his head, a dream in which
he saw himself eyeing his father there
at the firelight's edge — the boy angry
at being left alone to watch the horses,
and running against the old man with his fists.
It was a dream he willed and yet could not
control: always his father in the dream
would catch his wrists and wrap him in his arms,
and the boy, sobbing, had to catch his breath.
It was only a dream — no use to him.
He knew tomorrow, next day, sometime soon,
he'd hear the truck come rattling up the road,
just in time for supper, probably,
the old man getting out and glad to see him,
wiping his mouth on the back of his hand
in that absentminded gesture of his,
as casual as if he had been gone
an hour or two at most, and then he'd say,
"How's my boy?" and ask about the horses.

                                   Roy Scheele

Photo of Women Plowing
(circa 1899)

The driver's face has no features,
a dark day-moon
about eight women harnessed to the plow.
They do not look up or talk
of beauty wrapped in cotton.
They hide their eyes
in bonnets, nothing certain
but the driver, slow
and heavy-booted.
They know they are better than horses.
They have eaten silence
with chapped lips at table,
more bitter before son
or husband than this boss man.
His face blackens from too few words.

Under billowed skirts, soft
forms blur the ugliest field. Wind
melds with grain dust, and moths
fly up suddenly at night
when the women wash their legs
lifting them softly in the half
light behind the shed.

                    CarolAnn Russell

Uncle Adler

He had come to the age
when his health had put cardboard
in all of its windows.
The oil in his eyes was so old
it would barely light,
and his chest was a chimney
full of bees. Of it all,
he had nothing to say;
his Adam's-apple hung like a ham
in a stairwell. Lawyers
encircled the farm like a fence,
and his daughters fought over
the china. Then one day
while everyone he'd ever loved
was digging in his yard,
he suddenly sucked in his breath so hard
the whole estate fell in on him.

Ted Kooser

Not Much Unsettled or Disturbed

Joseph Sullivan was thirty-eight years old when he crawled under his combine to fix a broken sickle, leaving his three-year- old son in the cab. His son got bored, started to play with the levers and pedals, and dropped the combine onto his father's chest. I imagine a sigh, huge and compressed, of hydraulic oil moving through valves, perhaps a single creak of warning at the very instant of release, and then bones popping. When they found him, much later, they might have seen a look of growing surprise on his face—not much, and certainly not fear, there wasn't time for that, but something startled and mounting, something that might have been fear. Had there been time. And if they looked carefully.

But his wife found him, and family does not look carefully, not at times like these. Besides, there was blood coming from his mouth, dried and brown already, or at least I imagine there was, and blood is selfish, it draws attention to itself. So all she saw was blood, her husband's feet first, in thick, leather, lace-up boots, and she was screaming already. Though perhaps not; a combine header, the way it hangs out in front of the machine, looks light almost, airy. So she saw his boots but didn't scream. She thought: 'The combine header fell on Joe.' And she probably said: "Joe? Joe?"

And then she walked around to where she could see his face. And then screamed. And perhaps she tried to lift the header off of him, tugging at it with the superhuman strength of sorrow. It swayed, and Joe's head turned a little with it, looking first at her, then a bit away, then at her, then a bit away, surprised at her efforts, but not all that interested anymore. So when she was all done screaming, and worn out from trying to lift something that could not be lifted, she had to leave him there because she did not know how to start the combine. She was a city girl, and the talk around the town, in the church groups and the pool hall, was that she had never liked the farm, and so Joseph had always kept it distant from her. Some people said she was a snob, and others said that Joseph spoiled her, that some hard work would do her a world of good. But we all live our lives by compromise and adjustment, and there is no telling what she did and did not do, so these comments always bothered me, and I tried not to listen to them.

Of course no one was saying those things after Joseph died. She had to leave him and go back up to the house, stumbling, I imagine, over the cut wheat and chaff. She wasn't far from the house, and her oldest son should have heard her screaming, but I suppose the air conditioner was on or the television, or else he just didn't pay attention, having no part of his mind in which to place his mother's screaming. So she found him, and at first she couldn't speak, and he stared mutely at her, waiting. Then perhaps she said: "Your father. The combine." Probably not much more than that, but it was enough, and he was gone through the door, leaving her in the house to hug tightly the three-year-old, whom her oldest son an hour earlier had found playing alone in the cab of the combine and brought back to the house. The oldest son had been outside, I suppose, doing chores, and the child, bored now and unable to climb down by himself, had called to him across the hundred yards or so of stubble. And normally the older brother would have wondered about the engine running and the child alone, but breakdowns are common at harvest and he was no doubt exasperated with his younger brother, and he had machinery running himself, a silo unloader going or perhaps a grain bin nearly full, something that he had to watch, and so he sprinted across the stubble and grabbed the child and brought him back, too harassed by his own jobs to let the strangeness of that idling combine bother him.

It would have been too late, of course, even if he had found his father; everyone has told the oldest son this, and he says that he knows it himself. But I can imagine that in the back of his head there will always be a small uncertainty, a belief that he had the chance to save his father's life but did not recognize it, that things could have been different, but they are not. And the three-year-old: it was only after much patient questioning that they found out what had had happened. They tried to be calm, but no doubt he sensed something wrong, and at first may have denied that he was even in the combine cab. But eventually it came out. He was probably too young to make any connection between the questions they asked and his father's disappearance, and perhaps the whole family made a pact never to tell him, to spare him the guilt of knowing.

In any case, the combine was started, and the lever was pulled back, and the engine, with no noticeable drain in its power or rpm's, raised the header with a whirr of hydraulic fluid, and Joseph's eldest son scrambled down from the cab and ran around to the front, and stumbled, I imagine, and stopped, and then hesitated, seeing the crushed chest of his father, and did not know whether to return to the cab and back the combine away or grasp his father by the boots and pull him out from under the machine. Perhaps, caught between leaving his father again or touching him, he could do neither, and stood there or fell to his knees, and stared or looked away. But by then, no doubt, there was the sound of an ambulance siren, high and far away yet, over the throbbing of the pulsing machine.

Then it was out of their hands for a while. I see the ambulance

continued . . .

raising dust down the gravel road, flickering, rocking on its springs as it corners into the driveway, then stopping in front of the house, its siren ending in that odd, sudden, braking way of sirens. Then one of the men points, and perhaps something is said, and then the driver turns away from the house, hesitates, and drives into the stubble, bouncing over the ruts, through swarms of grasshoppers.

They did what they had to do because there was nothing else they could do, and returned over the stubble with Joseph, and the oldest boy in the passenger seat. And I have heard that Linda was waiting with the three-year-old near the front of the house, and she would not let the ambulance crew say no, so they all crowded in, and under flashing lights returned to town.

And when they came back, we were already in the house, waiting. Women had brought bread and hot dishes and other food, and people talked quietly, and there were hugs and tears. Someone had somehow learned that Joseph's daughter was shopping with a friend in another town, and had gone and somehow found her, and brought her back. And she waited, confused and overcome, the center of an attention she did not fully understand, until her mother came home. We sat and talked, and felt we could not leave or felt we should not stay. And in one of the long silences, when the tears had stopped and no one knew what to say or whether anything should be said, a sound became apparent in the house, and people looked furtively at each other, quickly sipped their coffee, cleared their throats. Then one of the men, nudged by his wife, got up and went outside. Minutes passed. People tried to talk. Then the diesel throbbing of the combine engine, which had been idling for hours, stopped. And when the man who had left came back in the door, everyone looked at him until he had taken his seat and was staring at the floor.

Then it was the mortician and the funeral director and the priest, and the tombstone salesmen, apologetic, but who had to make livings too. And two weeks after the funeral the editor of the local paper wrote a column about preventing farm accidents. Along with the usual advice that everyone knows and sometimes obeys, like staying away from moving parts, he also warned people not to crawl under machinery held up by hydraulics without first locking the hydraulic controls. And never leave a young child in the cab, he wrote. This column angered many people. "The man is dead," they said. "Why make an example of him?" And they had a point, I think.

Linda did not return to the city. Perhaps guilt kept her on the farm, or perhaps sorrow, or perhaps everyone had been wrong and she wanted to stay. But she did not farm. She rented the land out and sold all the machinery. At the auction, no one would bid on the combine. It was an old machine and often repaired, and there were stories that

Joseph had never been happy with it. And some people, I know, though they would not admit it, were bothered by the blood that might be upon it. So when the auctioneer went toward it they muttered and put their heads down and their hands in their pockets so that the auctioneer would not think that they were bidding.

So the combine was going cheap to a man from another county. I, too, was staring at the ground. But then I looked up, and off to the side I saw Linda, stone-faced but pretty, I thought, and young, and somehow alive in an immobile and worried sort of way. And the urge came upon me to bring her more money for the combine. So I jerked my head and raised the bid, and raised it again, and I would have stopped there but the stranger stopped before me, and so I found myself owning Joseph Sullivan's combine. I had not intended it. It was one nod more of the head than I had planned. But Linda was smiling, a brief smile directed right at me, and she brushed her hair back away from her face, and it was black, and her eyes were dark and bright, and she did not seem clouded with sorrow.

Time, of course, goes on. All this happened a year ago, the land has frozen and given another harvest, not much unsettled or disturbed. Seasons force routines, and most people have forgotten already. No one thinks of Joseph Sullivan's death.

But I do. I think of how events continue, and I think of possible futures. In one future, a terrible tension exists between the oldest and the youngest son, the oldest feeling guilty for not saving his father but knowing that it is really the youngest son who caused the death. Yet the youngest seems blissful in his ignorance and leads a normal life, while the oldest is haunted, at odd moments when he is most happy, with the thought of his father lying underneath that weight, perhaps moaning, perhaps calling weakly for help, while his son climbs up the ladder into the cab and climbs down with the three-year-old in his arms, and turns his back, and returns to the house.

Yet the youngest son is haunted with his own visions. He does not know where they come from or why, but he may have dreams, nightmares, he may sense an immense sorrow, a strange guilt that has no explanation, descending upon him, most often, perhaps, in the fall and associated with the musty smell of ripe wheat and the slanting light of autumn.

But the oldest son does not know these feelings of his brother. So I can imagine that sometime in the future, when the family is all together, perhaps at Christmas or Thanksgiving, it will all come out. Someone will mention Joseph, and reminiscences will start, and the oldest son will feel this point of guilt growing in him. He will sit silently

continued . . .

while the others talk. Perhaps he will leave the room and come back. He will take a chair far from the others, hating to listen but not able to withdraw himself. And then the youngest son, in all innocence—he may be twenty years old now, or thirty—will ask some question about his father, and something about the question or about the way it is asked, something too naive and simple about it, will strike a spark in the oldest son's brain, and in a rush he will tell the story. He will say: "You killed him. He was under the combine, and you were three years old, and you were playing in the cab and you dropped the header on him. And we didn't find him until hours later. Not until hours later!"

And so it will all be out. There will be a stunned silence after this outburst, and the oldest son, in that silence, will know that he should have said nothing, and everyone in the family will know that they should have told the youngest son from the beginning. For now, in spite of himself, and in spite of everything they say and all the apologies from his older brother, he will wonder if the reason they never told him was because they really do blame him. He will feel ill-at-ease with his older brother, not knowing the older brother's own guilt. Thus, instead of sharing the strangeness of the world and their own ignorance of its ways, they will each take that ignorance upon themselves and add to guilt, regret.

But there are other futures also. Perhaps the oldest son is of another nature, more practical and less given to introspection, and all too aware of the heaviness of iron. Perhaps when he is told that there was nothing he could have done he believes it not only with his mind but also with his heart and blood. And perhaps the youngest son was told what happened and learned to accept it before he came to be able to think about it.

And there is Linda, too, who may have her own guilt and secret knowledge; she may have asked Joseph to take the three- year-old for an hour or two, or if not asked, consented. Yet even in this asking or consenting she may have felt foreboding, so that now she may wonder at her own innocence, perhaps even her own motives.

Any of these things might be true, and any degree of talk and sharing, so that Joseph's death leads to endless possible scenes, all of them tense, though some less so, and all of them stemming from what is known and what is not known, what is believed or not believed. And I wonder, too, at my own motives, not over Joseph's death, but over that smaller, later thing, and if there is a future in which my action will affect the story that I tell.

Perhaps there is blood under the header. Sometimes I imagine a red stain spreading and shaped like an amoeba, and I think that I should not have nodded my head that last time. I wonder why I did. But then I know that the stain is not there; the harvest has worn everything off, the stubble and dirt have scraped Joseph's blood clean, and if his blood is anywhere it is in the soil of the land that I own, somehow mixed up and irrecoverable. There are times when I am plowing in the evenings or mornings, when the light is still orange or red, that I glance back and think that I see that blood, turned up by the plow, a red glint in the sheen of the fresh soil. Joseph's death then is like a presence to me, welling up from the land. But I shake my head and tell myself that there is no need for this.

But when night settles on the land, softly, I think of Linda's black hair and eyes, smiling at me, and I wonder if she saw a connection that I was too dim to realize. I imagine her in her house with her children, attending to all the things that need attending to, doing dishes in the evening and staring out from her kitchen window at the land losing shape to the darkness, and living and waiting for the future to unfold into the present. Our paths never cross, but they might and they could. I wonder if she would smile again, or turn away, or not recognize me at all.

Kent Meyers

The Mexican Girl

The Mexican girl
in Clayton, New Mexico
smiled warm,
and I grinned back over
my wife's shoulder.

When she took our order
I thought to myself:
I'll take your dark eyes
under a desert moon;
I'll give up my rambling vows
for your small town perfumes.

It's sweet haunting
how longing,
a few booths,
stranger faces
and the jukebox
can move the soul
into intimate lonesome.
Hardly noticeable
the brown waitress
moving her hands
in the counter routines.

When I paid the bill
she said: come back.
Two soft words
I took back to the big sky of Montana
and whispered to the quaking aspens
of the Yellowstone River.
Come back: a dark-skinned lullaby
to share with the wild water
bulging at the spring banks.

Art Cuelho

Symptoms

At 61 she keeps falling
in love — often twice
in one day: the black
man who reads the
gas meter, the Zen Buddhist
who smiled, the Vietnamese
couple who bought the
delicatessen, the red-bearded
artist younger than
her son, an entire
woodwind quintet.

Her children drop their work,
rush home. This
is no fly-by-night change-
of-life symptom like the
poetry thing. This indiscriminate
falling in love reflects on
the whole family. They speak
in low voices as if attending
a sick bed, last rites.

                      She
answers the door — she is
falling in love
with the candidate for the
44th district. He leaves her
his picture.

Ruth Roston

Old Soldiers' Home

On benches in front of the Old Soldiers' Home,
the old soldiers unwrap the pale brown packages
of their hands, folding the fingers back
and looking inside, then closing them up again
and gazing off across the grounds,
safe with the secret.

Ted Kooser

Old Men's Hands in Their Laps

They sit there, staring out from the wreckage
of mute faces — old men who have lived,
whose wrinkles tell the story of their lives.
They are our grandfathers and fathers.
And now they are ourselves.

Dry husks that wither
in the slant light of October,
their one wish is to sit in the sun
and never move again — those huge hands
folded quietly in their laps.

Tom Hansen

Hands

they are always moving
in and out of my past

a grandfather's hand
circled with serge, holding out
a blue glass elephant
the other fist cupped over
a burled wood cane, both hands
moons of blue craters

a mother's chapped hands
draping wet sheets over a wire line,
the wooden pins like small ducks
swimming from her mouth,
the wind snapping the sheets,
the red fingers stretching
and smoothing

and the daddy's hands
just in from carrying
a chorus of milk bottles,
untangling dairy coupons from a wood box,
his head nodding at noon

the hands of the kitchen sister
at Sunset Home, prayerful hands,
soft cookie warm

but never,
never the old hands in the sun room,
hands resting on wicker,
reaching out to reel in
a four-year-old frame, drawing it
close to dim eyes to breathe
something young

Shirley Buettner

Hands

The words won't come right from my hands
in spring. The fields are full
of baby calves, tufts of hay, bawling cows.
My brain is full — but words won't come.
Sometimes when I'm in the truck,
leading heifers to spring grass, I find a stub
of pencil, tear a piece from a cake sack,
and make notes, listening to the curlews'
wolf whistle. A barb tore that knuckle,
when I shut a gate without my gloves. the blood
blister came when someone slammed a gate
on the branding table; I tore the fingernail
fixing a flat. The poems are in the scars,
and in what I will recall of all this, when
my hands are too battered to do it anymore.

Instead of a pencil my hands,
knotted like old wood, grip a pitchfork,
blister on the handles of a tiller. Slick
with milk and slobber, they hold a calf,
push the cow's teat between sharp teeth —
feel his sharp teeth cut my fingers —
another scar. My hands pour cake
for the yearlings, seed for the garden
to feed my family.

My hands become my husband's, weathering
into this job he chose by choosing me; my father's,
cracked and aged, still strong as when
he held me on my first horse. All night,
while the rest of my body sleeps, my hands
will weave some pattern I do not recognize:
waving to blackbirds and meadowlarks,
skinning a dead calf, picking hay seeds from my hair
and underwear, building fires. Deftly, they butcher
a chicken with skill my brain does not recall.

Maybe they are no longer mine but grandmother's,
back from the grave with knowledge in their bones
and sinews, hands scarred as the earth they came from
and to which they have returned.

When my grandmother was dying, when
the body and brain were nearly still
for the first time in eighty years, she snatched
the tubes from her arms. At the end,
her hands wove the air, setting the table,
feeding farmhands, sewing patches. Her hands kept
weaving the air,
weaving the strands
she took with her
into the dark.

Linda Hasselstrom

The Auction

Not even a bid
on the old plow
rusting in the grove.

We were married only months
when he took all our money
and bought that plow —

really all my money, money
I had earned as a hired girl,
babysitting, walking beans.

He didn't ask me,
just bought the plow.
Our first big fight.

His main fault maybe —
if something needed doing,
he didn't think about feelings.

I feel him behind me now.
He touches my shoulders in a way
that says he remembers

how much that plow cost.

Leo Dangel

The Junkman: From *Remembering the Soos*

There was a deaf and dumb junk dealer in our neighborhood, a wiry, heron-eyed, small-headed man who always wore a greasy black seed hat. We boys called him Deefy. He pulled his two-wheeled junk cart up and down our cindered alleys looking for anything he could sell, trade or hock. Useful, fabulous junk: bike tires and frames and chains, lamps, bathroom cabinets, mattresses, wagon tongues, hubcaps, over-stuffed or folding chairs, frying pans, flashlights, picture frames (empty or otherwise), vacuum cleaners, mirrors, doors, shingles, rakes, hoes, sinks, bird baths, saws, comic books. He hoarded everything.

We could hear the wheels of his cart crunching the cinders a block away. We loved to follow him, at a safe distance, and mock him and taunt him with insane gestures and words, especially behind his back. He knew the best way of handling us was to keep plodding straight ahead as if everything was normal; the less commotion the better. From a quarter of a block away we'd throw rocks *toward* him, never quite *at* him, but sometimes they'd *whang* off the back of his cart and he'd feel the vibration and suddenly stop. The cart handles would shoot up, he'd whirl around and nail us with an eye and scream an eerie, wild scream that scattered us like shotgunned rats down the alley, over yards, across streets, howling for joy. To him, his voice must have felt like a violent expulsion of air; to us, it was the rending of steel.

Sometimes we'd follow his bobbing seed hat all the way to his house—almost a shack—a block and a half down the street from my house, where he lived with his deaf and dumb wife. (They had a son our age, with normal hearing and speech, who lived with relatives.) There he'd lock up his loaded cart inside a wooden gate and go in, ignoring us more. So our rocks thudded on his plywood windows, on his front door. Or, if one of us was brave enough we'd sneak up and "ring" his doorbell, which was a light in his front room, and run back to the others, crouched behind some bushes. Tense and light-footed, we waited for the door to explode its hinges. He must have hated and feared us for our taunting, our rocks, our constant pestering that interrupted his meagre yet serious attempts at making a living. I think he would have loved to get his hands on just one of us for a lesson. But he never came out.

My fear of the junkman was not simply a piece of neighborhood mythology. It was more like xenophobia: deep and irrational. I had dreams of him chasing me down alleys, my legs and arms pumping in slow motion, his quick, jerky steps and wild grunts growing louder and louder behind me. Awake or asleep, I imagined him catching me with his wiry arms, squeezing my neck, screwing his thumbs in my eyes, screaming in my face like a maniac.

And then one night something happened that not even a dream could dream up.

I had been to a monster movie with a couple of friends and was jogging the three blocks home from where the bus had left me off. My friends had gone their own ways, I had only streetlights for company. My habit after dark, whether I'd been to a monster movie or not, was to avoid alleys, but this night I decided to push my fear a little. When I got to Strongin's grocery store, a block east of my house, I had three options: straight up the alley; around the block to the south, which would take me by the junkman's house—even though he'd no doubt be in bed (I'd never seen him out at night), I didn't like passing his house; and around the block to the north.

I decided on the shortest route and took off up the alley. Running full speed at night was dangerous because I couldn't hear anybody or anything above the sound of my footsteps, and yet I was too scared to slow down and listen. I was at top speed when I hit the intersection half way home, just as the junkman and his cart appeared and met me exactly in the center of the alley—we couldn't have timed the meeting better! At first I was more surprised than scared. Not missing a stride I veered sharply—a butterfly caught in a sudden blast of wind—nearly bumping the cart going around it, and continued my straight line home. The junkman had had even less time to react, since he was looking the other way. When he saw me he skidded, his cart handles flew up and he grunted, startled. I got to the end of the alley, took a rounded left, my momentum carrying me out into the street, and when I got to my house I jumped over the picket fence and was gone.

After that night I never again mocked the junkman. For both of us that sudden confrontation in the alley between our houses had been at the same time embarrassing and frightening. The incident, curiously, started a subtle bond between us—something close, that only lovers or best friends can feel. Literally and metaphorically, our lives had intersected. Whenever I saw him I regarded him with respect, and though he didn't smile, his face was changed.

A month or two later I got up enough nerve to take my father to his house to look over a skinny-wheel bike he had for sale at an outrageous price of ten dollars. I felt strange standing there several feet away from the man I had once tormented with rocks and gestures. He seemed congenial, decent, like the other men in the neighborhood, except that he was deaf and dumb and could only grunt. My father and he couldn't agree on a price—which they kept handing back and forth on slips of paper—but by the time we parted and the junkman's eye caught mine, I realized we were no longer enemies.

David Allan Evans

Christmas Eve

Now my father carries his old heart
in its basket of ribs
like a child coming into the room
with an injured bird.
Our ages sit down with a table between then,
eager to talk.
Our common bones are wrapped in new robes.
a common pulse tugs at the ropes
in the backs of our hands.
We are so much alike
we both weep at the end of his stories.

Ted Kooser

July

In hated towns, even, churches ring
their morning bells—at 8 or 9, maybe.
In summer, when a breeze floats the last of night-cool
north, bells ring on that same breeze,

reminding even the most hateful banker,
walking to work, on the farm
he grew up on, three fields away from the Methodist
chapel, and even a budding thug,

en route to slashing Harold Nystrom's
favorite hybrid rose, will notice a twinge
the first knelling makes
in his rib. His job is not to remember it.

Then musical air turns normal.
Any town continues to pay its bills and have its
accidents, while the nearly clean river
eats a slow way through the concrete floodwall.

Day will heat up. Something memorable
may or may not happen during the lunchtime
hustle: people have their seizures then,
or get engaged. Either way,

afternoon will begin to crawl
beneath its humidity, the black locust more
tropical-looking, passing trucks
more and more like the tireless engines

of wilt and misery. Just before 6,
businesses all closed, most people home
or playing softball, leaves will start
a new trembling. The coals

will almost be gray enough for the meat.
Reading the paper outdoors, one person will feel
cool. For a moment, tricycle sound will stop.
Bells will have started ringing again,

a kind of slow-moving front
gone after their minute, raining on both
the beautiful and the damned,
drenching everyone with sure, unexpected music.

Richard Robbins

Neighbor

Morning and evening a heron flies
to and from its fishing of the lake.
It notices the slow wall of the nest
you are making, stone by stone,
and observes that you never leave the ground;
if it thinks, it thinks
that you have built too far from open water;
if it expects, it expects failure for you;
if it remembers, it remembers the camp
of shellfish people two thousand years ago,
whose huts were also interesting,
who also sometimes shouted into twilight.

Charles Waterman

Gathering

My aunt put on her black shawl and took me
by my hand held up to her waist, and went down
the gravel path and over the plank bridge
with a shopping bag which she bent down
to fill with french beans and peapods and new
orange carrots smudged with soil. I could see
birds quivering among the yellow weeds, a ledge
bracketed to a tree with a hive perched
on it, and the neighbor, Mrs. Gee's clothesline
pegged with panties and a torn shirt flying,
and the gold bees diving between these flags
and the waving grass. My aunt, who was dying,
looked like a skull with straw hat and glasses,
and Mr. Sams, the railway policeman, with bags
of potato-peelings for his fat pigs
next door, touched his bald pink dome, said "How do!"
to her, winked at me. She rested a thin hand
sinewy on the clothes post and stared at the parched
vegetable tops in their straight flat rows
and the descending ridges of blue tree'd
hills across the water, and the brick ranks
of houses with slate roofs in which she'd tried
to keep on growing. It was a sunny
fall morning with warm gusts now and then that
fell away, and soon there came an old man
on crutches hobbling to his bees, a cat
on a gate, and women and children arched
over tending their delicate garden crops
all around the gaunt lady with her shawl
and polka-dotted bag of greens. And she
was smiling with wide black eyes, and her fingers
tapped on mine to the tune of the lazy birds,
blue among the leaves. This tune is one that lingers
when the brown roosters ruffle and stalk me,
and the old bees waver among the falling
apples. The blue hills sway, the land drops
off to black water, where yellow leaves
float circling slowly downstream, opened up
like quiet smiles and the eyes of fading lives.

Antony Oldknow

Nebraska

The town is Americus, Covenant, Denmark, Grange, Hooray, Jerusalem, Sweetwater—one of the lesser-known moons of the Platte, conceived in sickness and misery by European pioneers who took the path of least resistance and put down roots in an emptiness like the one they kept secret in their youth. In Swedish and Danish and German and Polish, in anxiety and fury and God's providence, they chopped at the Great Plains with spades, creating green sodhouses that crumbled and collapsed in the rain and disappeared in the first persuasive snow and were so low the grown-ups stooped to go inside; and yet were places of ownership and a hard kind of happiness, the places their occupants gravely stood before on those plenary occasions when photographs were taken.

And then the Union Pacific stopped by, just a camp of white campaign tents and a boy playing his harpoon at night, and then a supply store, a depot, a pine water tank, stockyards, and the mean prosperity of the twentieth century. The trains strolling into town to shed a box car in the depot side yard, or crying past at sixty miles per hour, possibly interrupting a girl in her high wire act, her arms looping up when she tips to one side, the railtop as slippery as a silver spoon. And then the yellow and red locomotive rises up from the heat shimmer over a mile away, the August noonday warping the sight of it, but cinders tapping away from the spikes and the iron rails already vibrating up inside the girl's shoes. She steps down to the roadbed and then into high weeds as the Union Pacific pulls Wyoming coal and Georgia-Pacific lumber and snowplow blades and aslant Japanese pickup trucks through the green, open countryside and on to Omaha. And when it passes by, a worker she knows is opposite her, like a pedestrian at a stoplight, the sun not letting up, the plainsong of grasshoppers going on and on between them until the workers says, "Hot."

Twice the Union Pacific tracks cross over the sidewinding Democrat, the water slow as an ox cart, green as silage, croplands to the east, yards and houses to the west, a green ceiling of leaves in some places, whirlpools showing up in it like spinning plates that lose speed and disapppear. In winter and a week or more of just above zero, high school couples walk the gray ice, kicking up snow as quiet words are passed between them, opinions are mildly compromised, sorrows are apportioned. And Emil Jedlicka unslings his blue-stocked .22 and slogs through high brown weeds and snow, hunting ring-necked pheasant,

continued . . .

sidelong rabbits, and—always suddenly—quail, as his little brother Orin sprints across the Democrat in order to slide like an otter.

July in town is a gray highway and a Ford hay truck spraying by, the hay sailing like a yellow ribbon caught in the mouth of a prancing dog, and Billy Awalt up there on the camel's hump, eighteen years old and sweaty and dirty, peppered and dappled with hay dust, a lump of chew like an extra thumb under his lower lip, his blue eyes happening on a Dairy Queen and a pretty girl licking a pale trickle of ice cream from the cone. And Billy slaps his heart and cries, "O! I am pierced!"

And late October is orange on the ground and blue overhead and grain silos stacked up like white poker chips, and a high silver water tower belittled one night by the sloppy tattoo of one year's class at George W. Norris High. And below the silos and water tower are stripped treetops, their gray limbs still lifted up in alleluia, their yellow leaves crowding along yard fences and sheeping along the sidewalks and alleys under the shepherding wind.

Or January and a heavy snow partitioning the landscape, whiting out the highways and woods and cattle lots until there are only open spaces and steamed-up windowpanes, and a Nordstrom boy limping pitifully in the hard plaster of his clothes, in a snow parka meant to be green and a snow cap meant to be purple, the snow as deep as his hips when the boy tips over and cannot get up until a little Schumacher girl sitting by the stoop window, a spoon in her mouth, a bowl of Cheerios in her lap, says in plain voice, "There's a boy," and her mother looks out to the sidewalk.

Houses are big and white and two stories high, each a cousin to the next, with pigeon roosts in the attic gables, green storm windows on the upper floor, and a green screened porch, some as pillowed and couched as parlors or made into sleeping rooms for the boy whose next step will be the Navy and days spent on a ship with his hometown's own population, on gray water that rises up and is allayed like a geography of cornfields, sugar beets, soybeans, wheat, that stays there and says, in its own way, "Stay." Houses are turned away from the land and toward whatever is not always, sitting across from each other like dressed-up children at a party in daylight, their parents looking on with hopes and fond expectations. Overgrown elm and sycamore trees poach the sunlight from the lawns and keep petticoats of snow around them into April. In the deep lots out back are wire clotheslines with flapping white sheets pinned to them, property lines are hedged with sour green and purple grapes, or with rabbit wire and gardens of peonies, roses, gladiola, irises, marigolds, pansies. Fruit trees are so closely planted that they cannot sway without knitting. The apples and cherries drop and sweetly decompose until they're only slight brown bumps in the yards, but the pears stay up in the wind, drooping under the pecks of birds, withering down like peppers until their passion and sorrow is justly noticed and they one day disappear.

Aligned against an alley of blue shale rock is a garage whose doors slash weeds and scrape up pebbles as an old man pokily swings them open, teetering with his last weak push. And then Mr. Victor Johnson rummages inside, being cautious about his gray sweater and high-topped shoes, looking over paint cans, junked electric motors, grass rakes and garden rakes and a pitchfork and sickles, gray doors and ladders piled overhead in the rafters, and an old wind-up Victrola and heavy platter records from the twenties, on one of them a soprano singing, "I'm a Lonesome Melody." Under a green tarpaulin is a wooden movie projector he painted silver and big cans of tan celluloid, much of it orange and green with age, but one strip of it preserved: of an Army pilot in jodhpurs hopping from one biplane and onto another's upper wing. Country people who'd paid to see the movie had been spellbound by the slight dip of the wings at the pilot's jump, the slap of his leather jacket, and how his hair strayed wild and was promptly sleeked back by the wind, but looking at the strip now, pulling a ribbon of it up to a windowpane and letting it unspool to the ground, Mr. Johnson can make out only twenty frames of the leap and then snapshot after snapshot of an Army pilot clinging to the biplane's wing. And yet Mr. Johnson stays with it, as though that scene of one man staying alive was what he'd paid his nickel for.

Main Street is just a block away. Pickup trucks stop in it so their drivers can angle out over their brown left arms and speak about crops or praise the weather or make up sentences whose only real point is their lack of complication. And then a cattle truck comes up and they mosey along with a touch of their cap bills or a slap of the door metal. High school girls in skintight jeans stay in one place on weekends and jacked-up cars cruise past, rowdy farmboys overlapping inside, pulling over now and then in order to give the girls cigarettes and sips of pop and grief about their lipstick. And when the cars peel out the girls say how a particular boy measured up or they swap gossip about Donna Moriarity and the scope she permitted Randy when he came back from bootcamp.

Everyone is famous in this town. And everyone is necessary. Townspeople go to the Vaughn grocery store for the daily news, and to the Home restaurant for history class, especially at evensong when the old people eat gravied pot roast and lemon meringue pies and calmly sip coffee from cups they tip to their mouths with both hands. The

continued . . .

Kiwanis Club meets here on Tuesday nights, and hopes are made public, petty sins are tidily dispatched, the proceeds from the gumball machines are talleyed up and poured into the upkeep of a playground. Johnson's Hardware store has picnic items and kitchen appliances in its one window, in the manner of those prosperous men who would prefer to be known for their hobbies. And there is one crisp, white, Protestant church with a steeple, of the sort pictured on calendars; and the Immaculate Conception Catholic church, grayly holding the town at bay like a Gothic wolfhound. And there is an insurance agency, a county coroner and justice of the peace, a secondhand shop, a handsome chiropractor named Koch who coaches the Pony League baseball team, a post office approached on unpainted wood steps outside of a cheap mobile home, the Nighthawk tavern where there's Falstaff tap beer, a green pool table, a poster recording the Cornhuskers' scores, a crazy man patiently tolerated, a gray-haired woman with an unmoored eye, a boy in spectacles thick as paperweights, a carpenter missing one index finger, a plump waitress whose day job is in a basement beauty shop, an old woman who creeps up to the side door at eight in order to purchase one shotglass of whiskey.

And yet passing by, and paying attention, an outsider is only aware of what isn't, that there's no bookshop, no picture show, no pharmacy or dry cleaners, no cocktail parties, extreme opinions, jewelry or piano stores, motels, hotels, hospital, political headquarters, travel agencies, art galleries, European fashions, philosophical theories about Being and the soul.

High importance is only attached to practicalities, and so there is the Batchelor Funeral Home, where a proud old gentleman is on display in a dark brown suit, his yellow fingernails finally clean, his smeared eyeglasses in his coat pocket, a grandchild on tiptoes by the casket, peering at the lips that will not move, the sparrow chest that will not rise. And there's Tommy Seymour's for Sinclair gasoline and mechanical repairs, a green balloon dinosaur bobbing from a string over the cash register, old tires piled beneath the cottonwood, For Sale in the side yard a Case tractor, a John Deere reaper, a hay mower, a red manure spreader, and a rusty grain conveyor, green weeds overcoming them, standing up inside them, trying slyly and little-by-little to inherit machinery for the earth.

And beyond that are woods, a slope of pasture, six empty cattle pens, a driveway made of limestone pebbles, and the house where Alice Sorensen pages through a child's World Book encyclopedia, stopping at the descriptions of California, Capetown, Ceylon, Colorado, Copenhagen, Corpus Christi, Costa Rica, Cyprus.

Widow Dworak has been watering the lawn in an open raincoat and apron, but at nine she walks the green hose around to the spiggot and screws down the nozzle so that the spray is a misty crystal bowl softly baptizing the ivy. She says, "How about some camomile tea?" And she says, "Yum. Oh boy. That hits the spot." And bends to shut the water off.

The Union Pacific night train rolls through town just after ten o'clock when a sixty-year-old man named Adolf Schooley is a boy again in bed, and when the huge weight of forty or fifty cars jostles his upstairs room like a motor he'd put a quarter in. And over the sighing industry of the train, he can hear the train saying Nebraska, Nebraska, Nebraska, Nebraska. And he cannot sleep.

Mrs. Antoinette Heft is at the Home restaurant, placing frozen meat patties on waxed paper, pausing at times to clamp her fingers under her arms and press the sting from them. She stops when the Union Pacific passes, then picks a cigarette out of a pack of Kools and smokes it on the back porch, smelling air as crisp as Oxydol, looking up at stars the Pawnee Indians looked at, hearing the low harmonica of big rigs on the highway, in the town she knows like the palm of her hand, in the country she knows by heart.

Ron Hansen

A Love Letter

Dry as everything in this year, I will not
be dry with you. Yes, I am farming. Would you
come to South Dakota? (None of this
is easy to say, nor is it meant to be.)
But come to me: the grass will be greener, the light
will make that shadow on your cheek you once
were proud of, and nothing will hurt you here. Come out
to me. (Good bones aren't given to all of us;
you should be proud.)
                            The rattlesnakes are neither
so big nor so common as people say. I shot one
yesterday, the first I've seen this year,
and hung it by the badger on the wall
of the sweetsmelling barn—that's just a custom here,
to make trophies of all your smallest enemies. The wheat
sprouted last week; without rain, it will burn away;
even so, we'd get along.
                            Will you come?
The deerflies are dancing a halo in the still air
by those ripe, gutted animals. Is your hair still blonde?
Or blonde again? (Yes, of course, I knew
that secret, anyway.) After all, maybe,
you'd like it here. The barn really does smell sweet;
you get used to the wind. Wait. . . that isn't so;
everything else, you get used to; no one
gets used to the wind.
                            But, you see, I hold you
to no promises. I wish you would come to me
here. We will lie in the dry grass, in the cloudless light;
"Will it rain?" you will ask, and "Yes," I will answer,
"I think it will."

                                    David Dwyer

Mulch

A mulch is a layer of organic matter
used to control weeds,
preserve moisture,

and improve the fertility of the soil.
You will not find naked soil
in the wilderness.

I started cautiously: newspapers,
hay, a few magazines;
Robert Redford stared up
between the rhubarb and the lettuce.

Then one day, cleaning shelves,
I found some old love letters.
I've always burned them, for the symbolism.
But the ashes, gray and dusty as old passions,
would blow about the yard for days
stinging my eyes,
bitter on my tongue.

So I mulched them:
gave undying love to the tomatoes,
the memory of your gentle hands to the squash.
It seemed to do them good,
and it taught me a whole new style
of gardening.

Now my garden is the best in the wilderness,
and I mulch everything:
bills; check stubs;
dead kittens and baby chicks.
I seldom answer letters; I mulch them
with the plans I made for children of my own,
photographs of places I've been
and a husband I had once;
as well as old bouquets
and an occasional unsatisfactory lover.

Nothing is wasted.

Strange plants push up among the corn,
leaves heavy with dark water,
but there are
no weeds.

Linda Hasselstrom

Composting

Throw in a little bit
of everything:
outer leaves of artichoke,
outrageous old potatoes,
young sparrows flung
by spring's caprice
to unceremonious death,
even heart and head
of unsuspecting gopher
compliments of the cat,
and finally, clippings of hair
dark and fair
from your husband's
and children's heads
absurdly beautiful,
fashioned like fruits
of the gods,
knowing here,
midway in your life,
how everything moves
towards one fine heap
one broken breathing
corpse of blood, brain,
husk and shell
which could,
if we only willed,
replenish this earth.

Florence Dacey

So This is Nebraska

The gravel road rides with a slow gallop
over the fields, the telephone lines
streaming behind, its billow of dust
full of the sparks of redwing blackbirds.

On either side, those dear old ladies,
the loosening barns, their little windows
dulled by cataracts of hay and cobwebs,
hide broken tractors under their skirts.

So this is Nebraska. A Sunday
afternoon; July. Driving along
with your hand out squeezing the air,
a meadowlark waiting on every post.

Behind a shelterbelt of cedars,
top-deep in hollyhocks, pollen and bees,
a pickup kicks its fenders off
and settles back to read the clouds.

You feel like that; you feel like letting
your tires go flat, like letting the mice
build a nest in your muffler, like being
no more than a truck in the weeds,

clucking with chickens or sticky with honey
or holding a skinny old man in your lap
while he watches the road, waiting
for someone to wave to. You feel like

waving. You feel like stopping the car
and dancing around on the road. You wave
instead and leave your hand out gliding
larklike over the wheat, over the houses.

Ted Kooser

On Warm Summer Nights

On warm summer nights he walks to the silo to sing.
While the barn slowly sinks into itself, the silo is tall and
strong and still the perfect place to sing.
He brings white candles and some matches and climbs
into the silo, empty now since most of the cows were sold.
He lights a candle, pushes it into the packed silage, and
begins to sing quietly.
The sounds of old hymns ascend to the roof of the silo.
Sounds that soar forty feet into the air and return to surround
him like the pines deep inside the woods. There is no sound
like the sound of a silo singing.
His voice carries outside to the hills, into the woods,
across the lake, where it joins with the sound of the bared
roots of old oaks, the sound of corn squeaking in the garden,
the sound of two sorrel mares standing close, the sound of
pine needles dropping, the sound of jumping fish.
On a night like this he brings a good supply of candles.

David Bengston

Wedding Song

I will

live with you
blessed
with reason
and rhyme.

Say with you
worlds unsaid;
pray with you
for plain words.

Strong of eye,
cry with you;
happy mouth
laugh.

Fire upon flame
rage with you,
may blue rain follow.

Wing over wing
wrap you
to my breast
at evening.

Sigh over sigh
match the wind
in absent
presence.

Wish for wish
wake you,
want for want
take you.

Try for try
push on ahead,
following your ghost
into the wilderness.

Old song after old song,
I'll sing for new weather—
sing of new shapes
for unchanging love.

Freya Manfred

Sunday Morning

Now it is June again, one of those
leafy Sundays drifting through galaxies
of maple seeds. Somewhere, a mourning dove
touches her keyboard twice, a lonely F,
and then falls silent. Here in the house
the Sunday papers lie in whitecaps
over the living-room floor. Among them floats
the bridal page, that window of many panes,
reflecting, black and white, patches of sky
and puffs of starlit cloud becoming
faces. On each bright brow the same light falls,
the nuptial moon held up just out of sight
to the left. The brides all lift their eyes
and smile to see the heavens stopped for them.
And love is everywhere. Cars that have all week
lurched and honked with sour commuters are now
like smooth canoes packed soft with families.
A church bell strides through the green perfume
of locust trees and tolls its thankfulness.
The mourning dove, to her astonishment,
blunders upon a distant call in answer.

Ted Kooser

Getting Physical

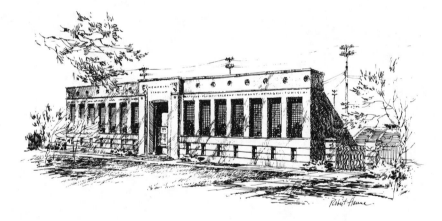

I n a poem called "Eagle," the contemporary writer Douglas Worth
describes how a parent bird pushes his young into the top of a tree,
leaves them there, and watches from a distance

> for panic and hunger to toughen
> their reluctant sinews
>
> then drives them screaming
> into their lives.

The young birds are not eagles until they leave the branches to which
they are clinging. In taking flight, they become themselves.

How do humans become themselves? Certainly through
what we sometimes refer to as "the life of the mind." We are thinking
beings who learn through contemplation and reflection. But we also
learn by doing, as Theodore Roethke says in a poem called "The
Waking":

> Great Nature has another thing to do
> To you and me; so take the lively air,
> And, lovely, learn by going where to go.

Learn by going where to go. That idea is also dominant in Alfred Lord
Tennyson's "Ulysses," his poem about the Homeric hero whose iden-
tity is created through movement. These famous lines are a summary of
Ulysses' being:

> I am a part of all that I have met;
> Yet all experience is an arch wherethrough
> Gleams that untravelled world whose margin fades
> For ever and for ever when I move.
> How dull it is to pause, to make an end,
> To rust unburnished, not to shine in use!

Walt Whitman said very similar things in "Song of Myself," his long
poetic celebration of physical and spiritual experience. Here is his
advice to a hesitant young man:

> Long have you timidly waded holding a plank by the shore,
> Now I will you to be a bold swimmer,
> To jump off in the midst of the sea, rise again, nod to me, shout
>   and laughingly dash with your hair.

Yet Whitman also knew that participation should be combined with reflection. "I take part," he wrote, but to that he added "I see and hear the whole." He acted, and he thought about his actions. He obviously believed in an integrated state of being, the lifestyle now referred to as "holistic."

But what is the best mind and body combination? While it can be argued that an almost purely cerebral existence can be physically unhealthy, it can also be argued that unthinking action can dull rather than heighten our mental awarenesses. How does one achieve balance? Whitman's answer to that question is contained in one of his best known lines:

"I am the poet of the Body and I am the poet of the Soul"

Whitman's means of integration was language. Through his art, his muscular words, he realized the world he was experiencing. His poetry, like much of literature, is in important ways physical. The right words are energizing. They make things happen, and they are themselves happenings. Because Whitman's poetically intense "Song" was both an expression and a continuation of his experience, his experience can become our own. Through the right words of artful writers, and through finding our own voices, Whitman would say, we can name the world and better understand ourselves and the meanings of the physical lives we live.

For example, consider "Football," the first work in this section. Through intense language and dramatic comparisons, metaphors, the poet delivers the violence of one of our most popular games. "Violence" is an abstract word, image-less, but the poet makes it vividly concrete by giving us "the bear with crushed face advancing." As we imagine groping for stones to throw with the primitive beings in the poem, re-created violence translates into understanding. Now, through verbal experience, we know. Just as we know the mind-altering terror of electric shock through "Pigeons," the work which follows "Football".

The other works in this section, while not always as dramatically intense as those first examples, are also explorations of physical experience and of what can be learned through that experience. They are generally arranged in a chronological order, from youth to age. "Pasttime," like "Pigeons," is about a child's early physical adventures, what are sometimes called initiation experiences. In that poem, the player on third is typical of the total involvement and egocentricism of childhood. In her mind, she is in the center of the world, the dramatic focus of the only game there is.

The next poem, "Handicapped Children Swimming," is another angle on exploratory experience.   The children in that still water have fewer physical resources than their "normal" peers, but they may be more imaginatively sensitive to the experiences they are capable of having.   Through the adversity of their physical limitations, they might be better able to imagine "Walking Through A Wall," the next poem in the section.

The poems which follow that one, "Bicycle" and "Out-And-Down Pattern," are voiced by loving parents who feel the typical ambivalence of wanting their children to learn to move on their own while fearing for them and regretting the loss of close contact.   These poems are also good examples of how basic physical actions can have many symbolic implications.   As is the case with most of the other writings in this section, the actions in these poems are both literal and figurative. They are metaphorical.

The same is true of the next three works. In the first of those, "The Touchdown in Slow Motion," the remembering athlete now knows that his exertions were for his watching parent as well as for himself, and he realizes that those actions had many implications beyond the schoolboy game he was playing. In "Rising From This Flat Land," the energetic sprinter, this time seen from a much greater distance, also implies meanings far beyond his competitive event, as do the young runners of "Beyond the Finish Line."

"Polevaulter" is similarly suggestive. It is also a close examination of the *process* of physical experience.   Against the frequent societal emphasis on the outcome, the results, this poem urges careful attention to the details of the event it describes. In implying the importance of patience, timing, and mental discipline, it presents a powerful argument for thinking action.

The next works in the section, "The Outfielder" and "We Cannot Save Him," are ominous warnings of the dangers of obsession. The athletes in these stories are focussed on physical experience at the expense of other things, including relationships with people who care about them. Because they are too singularly physical, they are endangered.   There are signs that the outfielder may finally be able to accept change, extend himself beyond his game, and be saved from his obsession, but in the other story the human cause seems lost.

In contrast, the two works which follow those are full of acceptance of the physical effects of time.   In "Village Softball League," there is the sadness of the loss of big league dreams, but there is also the bright promise of family and the next generation of participants.   There will be life beyond the game.   "Town Team" is a comic version of the same scene. Beyond obsessions with individual achievements and with winning, there can be pure participatory enjoyment.   What remains for these players may well be the best of their game: its vividly imagined grace, its bright ritual, its poetry.

Finally, "Escape From The Nursing Home" dramatizes the extreme difficulty of adjusting to the even greater losses of our physical selves which occur in old age. Even more dramatically, the poem's powerful images of coldness and darkness imply that which we must all eventually accept: the death which will be the final physical event of each of our lives.

Football

Consider the stoning of beasts;
the peppered mammoth slobbering in the pit,
the stunned boar,
the bear with crushed face advancing,
the crippled skirling cat;

consider the hands
groping along the hacked shores of rivers
how many dawns ago? for this shape of stone.

David Allan Evans

Pigeons: From *Remembering the Soos*

The two of us, at 14, stood there between the railroad tracks looking straight up at a piece of sun clearing the white east wall of the Nutrena Soybean mill. The mild shade was growing higher and higher up the wall, and just as the sun squeezed over, the noon whistle blasted.

We had plenty of time, and a good plan, and the men would be on the other side of the building eating lunch on the cool grass under the box elder trees.

Geesman was the lookout. I was the athlete, the climber. I patted my back pocket to make sure the pillow case was there. I was ready. From a pile of boards and railroad ties close to the wall, we grabbed a tie, each on one end, and slanted it against the building at a sharp angle, aiming for a window. I backed up several steps, then sprang forward onto the tie just fast enough to get my hands on the sill— held myself there a few seconds— then pulled up into the wide casing of the open window. I dropped down into the empty room, turned and stuck my head and arms out the window, and looked down. Already Geesman was holding up a long two-by-four from the wood pile. I took hold of the board, brought it through my hands, and slanted it crosswise in the window. I stood up on the sill and kicked some dried putty and splinters of glass off, for a place to stand in. I shinnied up the board high enough to get my hands on the sill directly above me. Then I pulled up into the second-story window, and dropped inside. My eyes weren't ready for the thick dark; I could see as far as two empty crates in the middle of the room. I turned around and looked over the edge at Geesman. He was waving up at me that everything was okay. I scraped some glass off the sill with my hand, and stood up in the clean spot. This time I didn't need a board—the steel rain trough was only a few feet above the window. I stretched until I got a firm grip on it, then jerked several times, testing its strength. I kicked my right foot up into the trough, hooked it with my gym shoe heel, and muscled up onto the roof, rolling over on my back on the warm, black asphalt.

For the first time, lying there, I heard the pigeons: a low dull cooing above me. I looked up in the direction of the sound. About 15 feet above me were two transformers on power poles side by side with some thick wires starting out of them. The lines were protected by a thin overhang held up by rafters, just above the top of the transformers. Between the overhang and the power lines, inside the rafters, were dark spaces. I knew the pigeons were in there. My climbing hadn't bothered them yet. They were still cooing and not flying around. I stood up quietly, and took one more look down at Geesman, who seemed no bigger than a doll, waving up. For a second I was light-headed.

The next climb had to be the quietest. I had to get on top of the overhang, then crawl far enough across it to be directly over the pigeons. I got up on an air vent, bear-hugged a transformer pole, and began to shinny up, slowly, carefully, to avoid splinters and to keep the birds cooing. When my head was just below the transformer, I shifted my weight onto a four-by- four a couple of feet from the pole, and kept climbing until I got hold of the overhang. I let my feet go, swung out free— hanging there a few counts—then pulled up on the top, rolling over several times to get clear of the edge.

Now, on my back again, I was above the birds, but still about 15 feet away. They'd heard the noise and had quit cooing. Four or five of them flew out over me, their white wings beating into the blue air. I lay quiet for a long minute. I listened to my pounding heart. Three birds came back, circled, landed on the lip of the overhang, and dropped down one by one between the wires, back to their shadowed nests. Apparently they hadn't seen me. I saw exactly where they went in. I waited another minute or so until I heard the steady low sounds, and then started crawling.

I stopped above the spot I knew they were under. I took the pillow case out of my back pocket and laid it beside me. I snaked forward silently, extending my head and chest over the edge. The overhang was unsturdy.

For some reason, I decided to test the wire that was close to the hole I would feel into. A wrist-thick wire wrapped with black tape. I reached down and touched it with my finger—*then I was dying—hung up by both hands on the wire—my neck screaming, bulging up close to explosion—currents of hot volts shooting up my legs, chest, arms—I was dying inside this electric second—seeing, feeling myself dying inside and outside my body—hung up by both hands—*

but then I dropped onto the roof, hard. Then my feet were more alive and lighter than ever, moving over the asphalt aiming for the place I had come out of on the roof before. Geesman must have seen my amazing vault over the rain trough, saw me getting bigger and bigger, the controlled fall, the swing into the upper window—legs, elbows, hands working in unison—the swing into the lower window, the sure-footed landing on the propped-up railroad tie, the leap to the solid ground— all this in a single, charged, unbroken motion. I whirled, crazy-eyed, and there was Geesman, back-stepping, speechless. All I said—three words—shot from my mouth like hot volts: *I got shocked.* My jaw collapsed on *shocked.* That word came out of my neck. Geesman kept

continued . . .

watching me, waiting for more words.

We started across the tracks for home, my steps still electric, avoiding the rails with ease, Geesman still watching my eyes. We climbed the steep one-block street and Geesman kept on going while I turned north on Wall Street, climbing the steeper hill that led all the way to the top of the bluff and my brick house. When I got there I walked around back and into the yard heading straight for the pigeon coop near the garage. I tripped the latch, opened the little door, reached in and lifted out a pigeon. I held it as high as I could and let it explode out of my hand. I reached into the coop again and again. One by one I lifted all of them out, held them high and let go, their white wings beating, beating into the steep blue air over Wall Street.

David Allan Evans

Pasttime

A girl, nine years of wonder
Still on her face,
Stands directly on the bag at third
Running amazed fingers along the wrinkles
Of my old leather mitt.
It is the bottom of the ninth
And everywhere in the world
The bases are loaded.

Emilio De Grazia

Handicapped Children Swimming

A measure of freedom. Mike, floating,
would not manage so without
the red life-jacket, but would sink,

messy as weed; but with it
lies, weak, like a shirt,
and the eyes, and the tongue

uncontrolled, extended, show
the delight it is to be
horizontal on water, strapped there

by nothing but sunlight. Connie,
who otherwise moves with crutches
and stiff braces, is strong

through water. Becky, seeing always
badly, lies washed by the sense
of her own fragility, liking

the help of warm hands. Gregg
rides and plucks at the water
while Danny makes his own music

in his mind as he lilts
completely quiet. Mikes' delight
opens like a flower as he floats.

He doesn't know he is floating
now in this poem. I have
nothing in fact to sustain him

and I know he will never stand
up alone. But whatever sustains
the children here is important;

inflamed with the success
of water, released, they mingle
and soften there, as wax

continued . . .

on wetness, limp as wet bread
on water's kindness. Those fingers
can grasp as competently at air

and water as mine. Their bodies
are milky and do not need
cleansing, except from deformity.

Water cannot wash their
awkwardness from them, water is
simple, and their defects difficult;

but they float for a while, never
as free as the times they fly
in dreams, over the cliffs

harvesting in the sea, the bats
exquisite with radar, but
something, a measure of freedom.

And Mike is lucid on water,
still physically cryptic, physically
glinting, but Mike has grace

for a while, this is his best
floating since before birth,
where he lay bunched like any

other unformed—encircled, contained,
his mother not knowing the
uncontrol of those limbs that

threshed and kicked at her
from out of that orchard of water.
Light queues to be present

as these imperfect children
float, perched rolling on
the foliage of water, shredded,

thick as May, shifting to new
flowerings of face, though their
limbs are weeds. Sunlight

strolls among them, padding,
healthy, firm, as our hurt
weak fleet gently disturbs the

soft clock of water. The shock
comes when you see the muscular
men who played with them

in the pool carry them
in huddles from the pool, sunlight
spreading its crime on them.

Michael Dennis Browne

Walking Through a Wall

Unlike flying or astral projection, walking through walls is a
totally earth-related craft, but a lot more interesting than pot
making or driftwood lamps. I got started at a picnic up in
Bowstring in the northern part of the state. A fellow walked
through a brick wall right there in the park. I said, "Say, I want
to try that." Stone walls are best, then brick and wood. Wooden
walls with fiberglass insulation and steel doors aren't so good.
They won't hurt you. If your wall walking is done properly both
you and the wall are left intact. It is just that they aren't
pleasant somehow. The worst things are wire fences, maybe it's
the molecular structure of the alloy or just the amount of give in
a fence, I don't know, but I've torn my jacket and lost my hat in
a lot of fences. The best approach to a wall is, first, two hands
placed flat against the surface, it's a matter of concentration and
just the right pressure. You will feel the dry, cool inner wall
with your fingers, then there is a moment of total darkness
before you step through on the other side.

Louis Jenkins

Bicycle

I shove my kid off
on his bike
for the first time
this time he
is able to go it
alone and he
begins miraculously
to understand balance
and I run alongside
helping, coaching, yelling
instructions, recriminations
afraid of all that lies ahead.

Greg Kosmicki

Out-and-Down Pattern

My young son pushes a football into my stomach
and tells me that he is going to run
an out-and-down pattern,
and before I can check the signals
already he is half way across the front lawn,
approaching the year-old mountain ash,
and I turn the football slowly in my hands,
my fingers like tentacles
explorng the seams,
searching out the lacing,
and by the time I have the ball positioned
just so against the grain-tight leather,
he has made his cut downfield
and is now well beyond the mountain ash,
approaching the linden,
and I pump my arm once, then once again,
and let fire.

The ball in a high arc
rises up and out and over the linden,
up and out and over the figure

that now has crossed the street,
that now is all the way to Leighton Avenue,
now far beyond,
the arms outstretched,
the head as I remember it
turned back, as I remember it
the small voice calling.

And the ball at the height of its high arc
begins now to drift,
to float as if weightless
atop the streetlights and the trees,
becoming at last that first bright star in the west.

Late into an early morning
I stand on the front porch,
looking into my hands.

My son is gone.

The berries on the mountain ash
are bursting red this year,
and on the linden
blossoms spread like children.

William Kloefkorn

The Touchdown in Slow Motion

The way to turn thirty
Is to kill off the light
And begin over
In slow motion:

So here I go
    in the shape
of my father's hope
    on a 30 sweep right
ranging out   cutting
    now turning it on
turning the corner
    to give up turf and
snatch what I
    need to be nifty
with a last fake
    in a farewell wave of my hand

stretching out
    I find my light
and a way to move
    in the green world

David Allan Evans

Rising From This Flat Land

Near Cozad a blazing white elevator
climbs one side of the sky.
Two steeplejacks straddle wind
to paint "Co-op" on the white crown.

Below, the grain broods,
dreams of barges bumping ice
on the Missouri.

A flock of sandhill cranes
lifts silvering bellies
just south of a snow flurry.

At the edge of Overton
a sprinter poises before
gun crack. His legs snap open,
soar over hurdles, stretch to
the highest rise in Dawson County.

Shirley Buettner

Beyond the Finish Line

Deeply tanned, elegant
bodies of country
boys and girls

            bounce

before the set
starting blocks.
Shake their feet,
twist their necks,
take their marks.

They are fragments
of the living sun.
Their eyes burn
coldly toward a distant
finish line.

We wait, then,
in the eternal
moment before explosion.
Such total dedication
to winning
is a game
of loss.
such intense desire

continued . . .

consumes our planet.

Who can tell them this?
Surely not those who drive them
like nails   into our future.

Who can tell them
that to be   bouncing
bits of the sun
is to be   far beyond
the finish line
before ever the gun
has barked?

Ah, they're off.
Good luck,
to all of us.

Joe Paddock

Pole Vaulter

The approach to the bar
is everything

unless I have counted
my steps   hit my markers
feel up to it   I refuse
to follow through
I am committed to beginnings
or to nothing

planting the pole
at runway's end
jolts me
out of sprinting
I take off   kicking in
and up   my whole weight
trying the frailty
of fiberglass

never forcing myself
trusting it is right
to be taken to the end
of tension   poised for
the powerful thrust to
fly me beyond expectation

near the peak
I roll my thighs inward
arch my back   clearing
as much of the bar as I can
(knowing the best jump
can be cancelled
by a careless elbow)

and open my hands

David Allan Evans

The Outfielder

1

What I like most is the room to move, room to flow until I'm under the high flies, waiting for their whiteness to cover my palm. There's a beauty in the outfield, a grace. Out here, no one touches you. You throw long pegs to second or home, but these are the only lines of connection. No one seems to know what I mean, to love it as much as I do. The woman I love understands it, but not completely. I try to tell her about it, but there are times when, like the flag stiffening on the center field flagpole, she pulls away from me and doesn't want to listen.

2

The woman I love tells me, look out into the world. Look beyond your self, your game. I love her for saying that. If she didn't say things like that, I would never love her. Still, she doesn't really know what I mean by the beauty of the soft cropped green outfield.

We drive in cars a lot. Sometimes she talks to me, sometimes she doesn't. She never talks outfield. She purposely avoids talking outfield. She thinks I get enough of it during the games themselves. Sometimes she talks houses: kitchens, sunlight sliding through the slats in the blinds, homes. What we could have between us. She never talks outfield. How I love that game.

Sometimes we stand in kitchens and talk for hours. The floors are green and clean, and I brush my toe across the tiles. Sometimes we sit at a diamond-shaped table. Lifting my coffee to my lips, I look up at the walls. Just don't let it be everything to you, she says. How I love the way she says that: her strength, the way the words leap out at just the right moment.

3

She agrees with me when I say I'm lucky I'm not an infielder. Lucky I'm not a shortstop or third baseman, those guys who can take no more than three or four steps before they dive for the hard grounders. I can't stand the feeling of dirt beneath my cleats. Sometimes they look face to face with line drives that, if they hit you in the chest, would shatter your heart like a window. I'm glad I'm not a catcher, held stiff behind mask and shin guards, a crouched crustacean. Glad I am not a pitcher, tearing my arm out by its roots while batters try to send each pitch flying to the moon.

Learn to be fast, I always told myself as a kid. Never be slow, or they'll stick you in the infield. I impressed them with the way my feet did not seem to touch the grass when I ran. Now, as a veteran, I must fight every day to keep my legs young.

4

Fans, she says. Fans are only superficial. They never love you the way I love you, she says. And I know it's true. She reminds me the fans don't know the real me, don't see me in the mornings, dropping my peanut butter toast to the kitchen floor. They have my photographs, touched up just right so they can't see the shadows, the time lines under my eyes. They don't see the chalky color of my face when I wake too early, my timing off, my timing off.

The fans love me, in their way. And I love them. Sometimes the sound of their cheers is like pure sunlight in my ears. But the fans only admire me in my white pinstriped uniform in center field under the floodlights; they don't see my shadow. I do, she says, and her timing is just right as she rounds her lips to say the words, just like a practiced umpire saying, "Strike two." I stand up from my side of the table, brush her hair back with my glove hand, touch her cheek with my bare hand.

5

An outfielder has a certain liking for fences, walls. Walls seem to contain you better than open fields do. You might say I am a little in love with walls. They let you know your limitations, they speak strongly to your shoulders when you back into them. Sometimes they outline my life.

They stop those line drives between center and left that skip by too quickly for any human to reach. They send the ball careening off, skimming toward you, so you can barehand it and nail the runner trying to stretch it to third.

I love to play the wall. Sometimes the true test is holding onto the ball you've just caught, even though you've hit the wall hard and everything hurts. The fences make the game.

A high fly to deep center excites me more than a pop up that I only have to take a step or two to catch. I love the wait, back to the fence, as the ball approaches, high and flying and spinning with all its strength. I love it when the ball finally comes down out of orbit. Just out

continued . . .

of reach, everyone says, just over the center field fence. Then the leap. The stretching of tendons. And I come down with a smile of white leather in my web, so bright it stings the batter's eyes.

6

The night she left me, the outfield grass felt like crushed apples, crushed apples, crushed apples.

7

Timing. Timing is everything. Timing is knowing where you will catch the ball even before the batter hits it. Timing is knowing when to dive for the line drive that's falling fast, it's knowing which shoe-string catches to go for, which are out of range.

If I drop a fly ball, I'm the only one to blame. Infielders can bobble a grounder, still throw their man out. With an outfielder, it's decisive: the fly ball cannot touch the grass or I die a little, right there in front of everyone.

Timing is everything when you're growing old. Timing is knowing the loss of a wasted moment, feeling its pain as you let it drop just beyond your fingertips.

Last night I dreamt of my first baseball glove. I used it for years as a grade school kid; it was a dark, leather glove with large, swollen fingers. I lost it somewhere in high school, but in my dream I slipped the glove on and the leather began to crack and flake. Then I tried to pull it from my hand but I couldn't. The crater-like pocket of the glove opened wide for me like a scream.

Timing is thinking about this long, high fly ball hit to center, this deep one that's backing me toward the wall. Timing is understanding this last deadly instant, with its correct spring of leg muscles, its reach, its squeeze. Thinking about it, ready for it. Yes.

8

A game isn't a game unless it's a close game.

Sometimes, when I'm standing out there, toeing the grass, watching man after man strike out or ground out, I think, let them get another run or two. Let them start some small fires.

What good is playing if it's not hit for hit, run for run?

What does winning mean if you always win by half a dozen? What good is winning if you never lose? Closeness. Closeness is everything.

9

The score is tied after nine innings.

I turn around between pitches and see her in the center field bleachers, watching me. Though she's never come to a game before, she's here; I can feel her eyes, like two heavy weights on my shoulders. Now's my chance to prove to her that I've never dropped one in my career, never.

The grass glows green beneath my cleats on this night, this game that has lasted long into the night until fans can see their breath in the moist August air. The beauty of it, I think as I watch the next pitch, then turn to her, the beauty.

I can't see the stars this night, even though I know the sky is clear and endless. The bright floodlights build a wall between me and the stars. I know she understands the outfield, she wants to be out here with me. Her face is white and clean as a new baseball.

Another out, another run for our team and we can all go home. They'll turn off these huge rows of blindness and we'll see the heavens again, we'll see our faces clearly again, by touch.

I turn again and she's gone. An empty hole in the bleachers where she sat. I can feel the lines etching deeper into my face, like grooves in the dirt of the dugout floor.

The hit rises from his bat. It's high and long to deep center. I race back and back at full speed, watching the ball over my shoulder all the while.

The ball begins its descent like a circle of light from a tiny spotlight, and it appears the ball is just out of reach. I time my leap.

Up. Full extension, my left arm stretched upward until all muscles scream. The glove opens hungrily, lovingly for the ball, the ball, the ball. From this height I think I can see the stars again. The fans are screaming like sirens for me, her voice screaming for me, for the game, for the outfielder.

10

Back at home we are sitting at the table in the green kitchen. We ignore all walls. She takes a sip of her coffee, then stands up. I stand up, slide around the table, and reach for her. With a pain that feels like flashbulbs popping behind my forehead I catch her in my arms and she embraces me and we hold on. We hold on. To everyone's amazement we hold on.

Bill Meissner

We Cannot Save Him

He was our friend, we miss him. But how were we to know when we laid our hearts in his hands, gave him our faith and admiration, that he would become what he is today, what we see already as we wait for him, half asleep in these dew-drowned bushes?

We miss him, who still unseen approaches, running with calculated prissy breaths above the foggy river. Before he rounds the brushy curve we see him, his French running shoes, his shorts, his naked legs, his T-shirt advertising something unimaginable. His terry sweat band, his stop watch, his tiny nylon wallet fastened to his shoe ingeniously with velcro, who once was never seen without a coat and necktie—hairy wool, rumpled linen, bleached-to-the-bone starched cotton broadcloth, stained shimmering reptilian silk—who hated zippers as much as polyester, snaps as much as leisure suits.

He was our friend, who traveled by a subway so dangerous and obscure that no one anyone knew had even heard of it, with whom alone we roared beneath the Mississippi, the ancient train crawling with the scum that cities full of hope and happiness generate according to some inverse law of social physics. With him we were horrified and unafraid. He was our friend, he led us clanking underground from the mildewed cavern of the old St. Paul Lower Market to the now-abandoned depths of the Fur Exchange in Minneapolis, and we miss him, who has a sticker on his car bumper, "I'D RATHER BE RUNNING," who has a bumper now, who hated cars.

We miss a whole elegant landscape of decay, the rich overlay of stagnation. It was he, himself, who pointed out the first faint trail parting the grass of the hitherto untroubled parkway along dotty, lilac-lovely Summit Avenue. We see him still, as he crouched suddenly under the lamplight, directing our attention to the barely visible spine of earth showing through the grass. We touched the packed soil uneasily where he pointed out the ominous ribbed print of an early clumsy running shoe. (This was before any one of us had ever seen a "jogger," but we had heard of them and knew what their spoor must mean.) We wanted to smash the bottles we were carrying home, to sow the path with glittering denial, but he smiled his disquieting smile and led us away, knowing we were lost. Later, when the path had doubled, then doubled again under the tread of runners, had grown into a freeway of sappy health, then we discovered our defeat's full depth.

We miss him, who understood the secret night squalor of these too facile, too habitable two cities, who recognized by voice and vice the fierce-smelling grizzled crocks whose slapping overshoes crunch down the frozen alleys behind loft-converted warehouses where city planners toast their luck with California wine, where young architects and MBA's and developers plot their clean and devastating lives over alfalfa sprouts and tofu.

He was our friend, we know he knows no fear and will not listen to the warnings we hopelessly recite: the jarred spine, ruined cartilage, wrecked knees and ankles, fractured shins, the mysterious sudden heart attack in the bloom of life, the neck broken on the expensive beach, the thugs waiting with chains and clubs in the inhuman unmoving early hours of morning. And we whisper to ourselves, he must not run along the river road at dawn, we cannot save him.

We miss him, he was our friend, who spoke intelligently in the smoking darkness of the last free lunch bar in South St.Paul, ripe with the reek of stockyards, spoke of Breton curb dancing, late Aztec erotic dentistry, the Parsee epitomes of the sixth century, who now subscribes to *Runner's World*, who jabbers eagerly about vitamins B and E, the relative merits of Tiger's Milk and Pro-Vita, about how good he feels about himself since he stopped smoking and drinking and eating red meat, who was our dark friend.

We have frozen in our heart's eye an image that humiliates and hardens our resolve: on the silent off-color television bolted above bottles, a mob of marathoners flows over the Lake Street-Marshall Avenue bridge, a river of specks streaming from nowhere to nowhere. Then, in close-up, we see him, captured randomly, neither first nor last, then gone, a number on his chest, who could explain with precision what went wrong with Horsley Beer after the retirement of brewmaster Koenigsberger and the ascendancy of Schlee, and who is now addicted to the mindless unsubtle high of oxygen starvation and pheromones.

He was our friend, we would warn him if we could. Any moment now he will appear, cheerful in his shorts and flashy shoes against the gray dead end of night, obliviously trotting towards us where we wait, miserable, hidden precariously, the Mississippi's bank sloping treacherously away beneath our feet, our sticks and greasy chains and lengths of pipe oppressive in our hands, warning silently, hopelessly: he must not run along the river road at dawn, he must not run along the river road at dawn, we cannot save him.

Lon Otto

Village Softball League

The larger but softer balls
rise in slow arches
between short baselines
like balled up, twined down
dreams of Yankee uniforms.

Somehow,
without planning it at all,
they grew up to be husbands and fathers
who pitch with fists
seamed with garage grease
or the irregular smudge
of pencils.

And yet, on plaid blankets
behind the snow fence
the petals of their women bloom.
And the pink buds of sunbonnets
nod on the heads
of their daughters.

The game is half over,
and the score is still zero.

Shirley Buettner

Town Team

The local jocks back home in Attica
seem more than amply snugged.

At first base a stomach extends itself
to scoop a low throw, like a gunslug,
from the dust.

The shortstop moves like a sweet fat fairy
to his right or left,
his sneakers leaking ballbearings.

Outfielders jog for several days to their positions,
pivot like bloated ballerinas,
doff their caps,
then jog for several days back to the dugout.

The infield is a squat and pussel-gutted chain.
Round faced and red, it
chews its tongue and
spits practically perfect daisies.

The pitcher trembles the mound with a headshake:
he wants another sign.
The catcher, wide as a sandcrab,
sweats marbles.

At the plate
a batter settles into his stance
like a tender, untapped keg.

William Kloefkorn

Escape From the Nursing Home

a woman
standing
naked

at night
in wet grass

in the back
yard

of a nursing
home

sees her
reflection

in a black
window

feels her
heart pound

sees her
white hair

sweep in
the cold wind

sees her long
shadow

alive on
the lawn.

David Evans, Jr.

The Wild and the Tame

L uther Standing Bear was born in 1868, the year of the signing
of the treaty which promised the Black Hills of South Dakota to
his people forever. Late in his life, Standing Bear said this about
natural places like the Paha Sapa, the holy hills of the Sioux:

> Only to the white man was nature a "wilderness"
> and only to him was the land "infested" with "wild"
> animals and "savage" people.   To us it was tame.   Earth
> was bountiful and we were surrounded by the blessings
> of the Great Mystery.   Not until the hairy man came
> from the east and with brutal frenzy heaped injustices
> upon us and the families that we loved was it "wild"
> for us.   When the very animals of the forest began
> fleeing from his approach, then it was that for us
> the "Wild West" began.

Much had changed in Standing Bear's lifetime, but by the time he
died in 1939, he had seen only the beginning of the change from
landscape to "manscape" which has been continuous since
then.   Here's what a biologist named Lewis Thomas has said about the
half century which followed:

> Where has all the old nature gone?   What became of the
> wild, writhing, unapproachable mass of the life of the
> world, and what happened to our old, panicky excitement
> about it?   Just in fifty years, since I was a small boy
> in a suburban town, the world has become a structure of
> steel and plastic, intelligible and diminished.   Mine was
> a puzzling maple grove of a village on the outskirts of
> New York City, and it vanished entirely, trees and all.
> It is now a syncytium of apartment houses, sprouting out
> of a matrix of cement flooded and jelled over an area
> that once contained 25,000 people who walked on grass.
> Now I live in another, more distant town, on a street
> with trees and lawns, and at night I can hear the soft
> sound of cement, moving like incoming tide, down the
> Sunrise Highway from New York.

Clearly, Thomas mourns the loss of his home place like Standing Bear
must have mourned the loss of the natural environment which was his
cultural home.
   Many other writers have similarly mourned the loss of place,
and continue to do so. Deep regret is implicit in these lines from a John

Dos Passos poem:

>...*the sixlane highway*
>*that arched the reedy rivers and*
>*skirted the fields of red clover,*
>*now in whine of windfriction,*
>*hiss of tires, valve-chatter,*
>*grumble of diesels, drone of exhausts,*
>*plunges under a rampaging bridge,*
>*sixlane under sixlane.*

And in a poem called "A Brook in the City," Robert Frost examined the environmental and possible human consequences of building a city over an energetic natural place.   The poem concludes:

>...*The brook was thrown*
>*Deep in a sewer dungeon under stone*
>*In fetid darkness still to live and run—*
>*And all for nothing it had ever done,*
>*except forget to go in fear perhaps.*
>*No one would know except for ancient maps*
>*That such a brook ran water.   But I wonder*
>*If from its being kept forever under,*
>*The thoughts may not have risen that so keep*
>*This new-built city from both work and sleep.*

Frost obviously believed that transforming certain landscapes might have negative effects on humans as well as on the wilderness.   In an essay entitled "Place in American Culture," Paul Shepard is even more explicit about the human cost:

>*Knowing who you are is impossible without knowing*
>*where you are.   But it cannot be learned in a single stroke.*
>*This is what makes the commercial ravagement of the*
>*American countryside so tragic—not that it is changed*
>*and modernized, but that the tempo of alteration so outstrips*
>*the ryhthms of individual life....*

But why has so much drastic landscape change occurred in recent years, if the negative effects are as easily observable as these writers say? An easy answer is of course that the reasons are economic.   Change has been necessary for "progress" and "growth."   Change is the inevitable consequence of mechanization

and industrialization.   But writers like Frost have suggested that there
may also be less obvious motivations.   Frost wrote that perhaps the
brook was submerged because it forgot "to go in fear."   Humans must
assert their dominance, "take charge," show nature "who is
boss."   Therefore, they *must* "tame" the wilderness.
    Closely related to that idea is William Faulkner's feeling that
another reason for "taming" has been human fear.   In his "The Bear,"
a story about a legendary wild animal, there is this description of the
dying wilderness and the great beast which still inhabits it:

> *...that doomed wilderness whose edges were being*
> *constantly and punily gnawed at by men with plows*
> *and axes who feared it because it was wilderness,*
> *men myriad and nameless even to one another in the*
> *land where the old bear had earned a name, and*
> *through which ran not even a mortal beast but an*
> *anachronism indomitable and invincible out of an*
> *old dead time, a phantom, epitome and apotheosis*
> *of the old wild life which the little puny humans*
> *swarmed and hacked at in a fury of abhorrence and*
> *fear like pygmies about the ankles of a drowsing*
> *elephant...*

That human fear of which Faulkner spoke is the subject of "The
Morning of the Wolf," a poem by a contemporary writer named Keith
Wilson:

> *The first time I saw him, he rose*
> *out of the grass of a hill, his eyes*
> *straight into mine, big head low*
>
> *He moved toward me, ignoring the man*
> *who stood beside me with the gun, his eyes*
> *straight into mine.   I was thirteen,*
> *taught to hate and fear wolves.   He, a lobo,*
> *a Mexican wolf from below the border.*
> *His eyes.   I keep coming back to that.*
> *The way they bore the center of me.*
>
> *The gun began firing, wildly, bullets*
> *splashing dust around the wolf but he*
> *barely moved, his eyes never left mine*
> *until I broke the contact and saw the man,*

> *his hands shaking, spraying the .22 bullets,*
> *caught completely in "buck fever," the wolf*
> *almost laughing, eased off through the grass*
> *his tail a contemptuous banner*
> *—his every movement sure of the morning, me,*
> *the long years I would remember his yellow eyes*
> *that big head looking at me.*
>
>   *I recall the smell of sage*
> *and creosote, the fear of that man, courage*
> *of the wolf.   Held in my brain, he never*
> *went away at all.   His footsteps sound outside*
> *my city window; his cry rises and falls*
> *on the dawn wind.*

In a poem entitled "Hurt Hawks," Robinson Jeffers also wrote about the distance between the wild and the tame, a distance which in his opinion has widened through time.   Speaking of "the wild God of the world," perhaps the spirit of the wilderness he loved, Jeffers wrote:

You do not know him, you communal people, or you have forgotten him;
Intemperate and savage, the hawk remembers him;
Beautiful and wild, the hawks, and men that are dying, remember him.

    The selections in this section are close examinations of these and related conflicts between the wild and the tame—conflicts which are perhaps especially frequent in this Great Plains area.   Here there are writings which celebrate the strength and mystery of the natural world, writings which describe the consequences of industrializing the landscape, and writings which explore the sometimes hurtful contrasts between the environmental philosophies of the first peoples in this area and more recent attitudes.   Implicit in most of these writings are the inner conflicts of individuals trying to come to terms with the many environmental issues and choices which are so integral a part of modern life.

    What are the implications of the frequently negative content of these and so many other contemporary writings on the subject of the natural world?   Perhaps these works are final commentaries on times which are past, and evidence that wilderness must inevitably be tamed, and give way to civilization.   Perhaps they imply that close experiential relationships with the natural world are disappearing and will soon be gone.

    Or perhaps they point toward hope.   Language, naming the

world, can be the beginning of change. Perhaps these writings are the beginning of a re-defining of relationships with the earth which could lead to the expression of a more sensitive and appropriate environmental ethic.

The Cat

All afternoon she's been out stalking.
Now she's dragged home the evening.
The back porch is littered with its feathers.

John Minczeski

Wolf

As soon as you say this word
snow begins to fall

W O L F

A shadow-word   undefined
as fog   it slips behind
sketches of dark pines
and birch trunks
its footprints quick
on the snowy page

W O L F

Whenever you say this word
a little girl fastens her red
cloak   and hurries along
the path

Muzzle turned
to the north wind
W O L F   runs
through the penciled woods
a winter moon
caught in its eyes

Barbara Esbensen

Flyway

A feather lifts
on the wind, and geese
fly in
from silent lakes
to stir the sky
above our field.

The morning air
beats against their thousand
wings.
It fills with their calls.

Now the sky tilts
and the geese pour down—
a heavy ribbon spiraling
into corn rows.

In the evening
under darkening air
the fields will lift up
on the wings of geese
and we will be alone
holding only a feather
against the cold.

Barbara Esbensen

Indian Boarding School: The Runaways

Home's the place we head for in our sleep.
Boxcars stumbling north in dreams
don't wait for us. We catch them on the run.
The rails, old lacerations that we love,
shoot parallel across the face and break
just under Turtle Mountains. Riding scars
you can't get lost. Home is the place they cross.

The lame guard strikes a match and makes the dark
less tolerant. We watch through cracks in boards
as the land starts rolling, rolling till it hurts
to be here, cold in regulation clothes.
We know the sheriff's waiting at midrun
to take us back. His car is dumb and warm.
The highway doesn't rock, it only hums
like a wing of long insults. The worn-down welts
of ancient punishments lead back and forth.

All runaways wear dresses, long green ones,
the color you would think shame was. We scrub
the sidewalks down because it's shameful work.
Our brushes cut the stone in watered arcs
and in the soak frail outlines shiver clear
a moment, things us kids pressed on the dark
face before it hardened, pale, remembering
delicate old injuries, the spines of names and leaves.

Louise Erdrich

Custer Cafe Eat

Shy Indian girl,
Her hands
do not know where they are.
Her legs
falter at the knee
like a pony's.

She walks

along edges
of tables.

Her faded
brown dress says
I am not here.
Her dark hair,
her skin, say
I am not here.

She stops, turns,
There
in her hair—
a bright
red ribbon;
and in her eyes
a dancing
like minnows in clear water.

Jim Heynen

Grandfather at the Indian Health Clinic

It's cold at last and cautious winds creep
softly into coves along the riverbank. At my insistence
he wears his denim cowboy coat high on his neck; averse to
an unceremonious world, he follows me through
hallways pushing down the easy rage he always has
with me, a youngest child, and smiles.
This morning the lodge is closed to the dance
and he reminds me these are not the men who
raise the bag above the painted marks; for the young
intern from New Jersey he bares his chest
but keeps a scarf tied on his steel-gray braids
and thinks of days that have no turning: he wore
yellow chaps and went as far as Canada to ride
Mad Dog and then came home to drive the Greenwood
    Woman's
cattle to his brother's place,

continued . . .

two hundred miles
along the timber line
the trees were bright
he turned his hat brim down in summer rain.

Now winter's here, he says, in this white lighted place
where lives are sometimes saved by
throwing blankets over spaces where the leaves are brushed
     away
and giving brilliant gourd-shell rattles
to everyone who comes.

Elizabeth Cook-Lynn

Burning

Every spring it is the same.

You come
with your can of kerosene
and your matches,
and I watch the thick smoke
welling up from the ditches,
the myriad orange tongues
lapping their hungry way
past my porch.

The fur-lined nests
crackle and stink,
the red eyes of rabbits
glow, and I hear
the smoldering cries
of their babies,
burning in their cribs.

Shirley Buettner

Winter-Kill

Long ears aim upwind.
December sun is
frozen in his eye.
He is hunched in the
last north acre
of the final field
where little game trails
cross and cross.

Someone is moving near
crouched   goggled
full tilt in the
Polar Cat—

He whirls to go
but the Cat
is *here above him*
with him   silvering
over blurring stubble
until his breath
bursts like a torch
and he runs down slow inside
giving a face to snow
giving   into it

David Allan Evans

Clinton Reservoir Displacement

The muddy new lake laps
over pastures and fields.

High over
an old windbreak
or a tree-lined creek
a few brown ducks
circle endlessly
around through limbs.
Tips of drowned elms
shape a last gesture
to the sun.

A gravel county road
slides straight
into the valley
full of water.
Farmers stand in hip boots
twenty feet out
solid on the road bed
casting and casting for bass.

Denise Low

Deer On Cars

deer on cars
on the freeways
move with an ease
and speed and courage
that seem beyond them:
when diesels scream by
they may jiggle
but it's never a leap
in a new direction
and more often
it is they
that pass the diesels...

entering a city
the head settles down
as they ease up in school zones
halt at red lights
or go on green
staring straight ahead
in the proper lane

David Allan Evans

Wasps

They were drawn to the shade
under the barn's eaves
and crafted a nest which hung
directly over the door,
so we killed them.

We filled a Folger's can
with gasoline, then flung it
onto their nest, drenching
the larvae packed away
like ammunition. The drones

fell, colors swirling
on their wings, marbled
like endpapers in an old book
boxed away in our attic,
a history of some war.

In its pages were lithographs
covered with fine, crisp paper:
young men died on the fields
in uniforms of blue, red and gold.

S. C. Hahn

Baling Wheatstraw on My 33rd Birthday

Between fallow and fallow, the mile-long strips
of stubble ten rods wide surrender
each from two hundred and fifty to four hundred
bales to the spring-steel fingers and close-
mouthed jaws of the loud, fast-talking machine.

Stubble-by, stubble-by, stubble-by-fallow, it says
in the light straw on the hilltops and *She wouldn't, she wouldn't,*
she won't, going down the draws. My old Eight-Forty
John Deere tractor asks me, *But wh'd'y'*
know? But wh'd'y' know? She might . . .
                                          Riding
the clutch in the thick bottom-land, I lose
all track of their talk, tractor and baler both chattering,
both snarling nonsense.
                        (A golden eagle helped me
seed this field last spring and ate the mice
and gophers I uncovered; now a misguided
sea-gull follows me, an easy symbol
of exile and high hopes.)
                        Hopes, the tractor
mutters, beginning to climb the draw. *Hopes,*
slopes, ropes, learn the ropes. The baler
answers: *Even . . . even the, even the, even the birds*
can fly.
The dead, the tractor snaps, *the dead, even the*
dead. . .Even the birds. . .(They have begun
to argue, it is so steep.) *Even the dead. . .*
Now, doesn't it? Even the . . .Doesn't it? Even the birds
can fly. Even the dead . . . But, doesn't it? doesn't it?
Even the dead can lie down. But, doesn't it? doesn't it
make you feel old? Well, you are. You are.

                                   David Dwyer

Rolla to Lawrence

Red-winged blackbird
dead on the road
six miles out of Rolla.
The body tells a story.

Opossum by the Gasconade River,
teeth bared in final fear,
motionless on concrete.

White cabbage moth,
wings flying flat and beautiful
on my windshield.

White and yellow cat,
fur catching afternoon sun,
I-70 past Columbia.

Something dark under vultures,
Blackwater, Missouri.

Roadside yellow with goldenrod—
sparrows wheel away just in time.

Near Turner
another stiff-legged dog,
a felled sparrow hawk,
wind lifting an empty wing.

Toward Lawrence
a dead coyote, yellow dog,
sun moving down flat and west.

Grackles lift off the road
rasping alarm,
dark shapes escaping into night sky.

Denise Low

Fort Robinson

When I visited Fort Robinson,
where Dull Knife and his Northern Cheyenne
were held captive that terrible winter,
the grounds crew was killing the magpies.

Two men were going from tree to tree
with sticks and ladders, poking the young birds
down from their nests and beating them to death
as they hopped about in the grass.

Under each tree where the men had worked
were twisted clots of matted feathers,
and above each tree a magpie circled,
crazily calling in all her voices.

We didn't get out of the car.
My little boy hid in the back and cried
as we drove away, into those ragged buttes
the Cheyenne climbed that winter, fleeing.

Ted Kooser

Klein's Amusement Show

I give him tickets for me
and my daughters, admire his black braids,
and we climb aboard the Tilt-a-Whirl.
Our faces are white with excitement.
He gives his machine the gun
and we fall into place.
I begin to feel like a book.
Or a dream.

He revs the engine once for Red Cloud
and then two fast ones for Sitting Bull.
We are flies spun into his web.
He lets us droop for a minute while he thinks,
then gives spin after accelerating spin
and slams my head back into the wire cage
for all the trees, rocks, rivers,
flowers and fish I have ever meddled with.
Now I know he wants to kill me.
And I want to get off.
I suddenly remember the story
of a girl who disappeared into the Ferris Wheel
somewhere in South Dakota.

But like a good spider he lets us go.
My feet smoke over the ground
like spirits of their former selves.
I avoid looking at him.
My kids think it was fun.
They say Momma has a weak stomach.
Later in the safety of my house
I think maybe he just wanted us
to have a good ride after all.

Cary Waterman

The Red Convertible: From Love Medicine

I was the first one to drive a convertible on my reservation. And of course it was red, a red Olds. I owned that car along with my brother Henry Junior. We owned it together until his boots filled with water on a windy night and he bought out my share. Now Henry owns the whole car, and his younger brother Lyman (that's myself), Lyman walks everywhere he goes.

How did I earn enough money to buy my share in the first place? My one talent was I could always make money. I had a touch for it, unusual in a Chippewa. From the first I was different that way, and everyone recognized it. I was the only kid they let in the American Legion Hall to shine shoes, for example, and one Christmas I sold spiritual bouquets for the mission door to door. The nuns let me keep a percentage. Once I started, it seemed the more money I made the easier the money came. Everyone encouraged it. When I was fifteen I got a job washing dishes at the Joliet Cafe, and that was where my first big break happened.

It wasn't long before I was promoted to bussing tables, and then the short-order cook quit and I was hired to take her place. No sooner than you know it I was managing the Joliet. The rest is history. I went on managing. I soon become part owner, and of course there was no stopping me then. It wasn't long before the whole thing was mine.

After I'd owned the Joliet for one year, it blew over in the worst tornado ever seen around here. The whole operation was smashed to bits. A total loss. The fryalator was up in a tree, the grill torn in half like it was paper. I was only sixteen. I had it all in my mother's name, and I lost it quick, but before I lost it I had every one of my relatives, and their relatives, to dinner, and I also bought that red Olds I mentioned, along with Henry.

The first time we saw it! I'll tell you when we first saw it. We had gotten a ride up to Winnipeg, and both of us had money. Don't ask me why, because we never mentioned a car or anything, we just had all our money. Mine was cash, a big bankroll from the Joliet's insurance. Henry had two checks—a week's extra pay for being laid off, and his regular check from the Jewel Bearing Plant.

We were walking down Portage anyway, seeing the sights, when we saw it. There it was, parked, large as life. Really as *if* it was alive. I thought of the word *repose*, because the car wasn't simply

continued . . .

stopped, parked, or whatever. That car reposed, calm and gleaming, a FOR SALE sign in its left front window. Then, before we had thought it over at all, the car belonged to us and our pockets were empty. We had just enough money for gas back home.

We went places in that car, me and Henry. We took off driving all one whole summer. We started off toward the Little Knife River and Mandaree in Fort Berthold and then we found ourselves down in Wakpala somehow, and then suddenly we were over in Montana on the Rocky Boys, and yet the summer was not even half over. Some people hang on to details when they travel, but we didn't let them bother us and just lived our everyday lives here to there.

I do remember this one place with willows. I remember I laid under those trees and it was comfortable. So comfortable. The branches bent down all around me like a tent or a stable. And quiet, it was quiet, even though there was a powwow close enough so I could see it going on. The air was not too still, not too windy either. When the dust rises up and hangs in the air around the dancers like that, I feel good. Henry was asleep with his arms thrown wide. Later on, he woke up and we started driving again. We were somewhere in Montana, or maybe on the Blood Reserve—it could have been anywhere. Anyway it was where we met the girl.

All her hair was in buns around her ears, that's the first thing I noticed about her. She was posed alongside the road with her arm out, so we stopped. That girl was short, so short her lumber shirt looked comical on her, like a nightgown. She had jeans on and fancy moccasins and she carried a little suitcase.

"Hop on in," says Henry. So she climbs in between us.

"We'll take you home," I says. "Where do you live?"

"Chicken," she says.

"Where the hell's that?" I ask her.

"Alaska."

"Okay," says Henry, and we drive.

We got up there and never wanted to leave. The sun doesn't truly set there in summer, and the night is more a soft dusk. You might doze off, sometimes, but before you know it you're up again, like an animal in nature. You never feel like you have to sleep hard or put away the world. And things would grow up there. One day just dirt or moss, the next day flowers and long grass. The girl's name was Susy. Her family really took to us. They fed us and put us up. We had our own tent to live in by their house, and the kids would be in and out of there all day and night. They couldn't get over me and Henry being brothers, we looked so different. We told them we knew we had the same mother, anyway.

One night Susy came in to visit us. We sat around in the tent talking of this thing and that. The season was changing. It was getting darker by that time, and the cold was even getting just a little mean. I told her it was time for us to go. She stood up on a chair.

"You never seen my hair," Susy said.

That was true. She was standing on a chair, but still, when she unclipped her buns the hair reached all the way to the ground. Our eyes opened. You couldn't tell how much hair she had when it was rolled up so neatly. Then my brother Henry did something funny. He went up to the chair and said, "Jump on my shoulders." So she did that, and her hair reached down past his waist, and he started twirling, this way and that, so her hair was flung out from side to side.

"I always wondered what it was like to have long pretty hair," Henry says. Well we laughed. It was a funny sight, the way he did it. The next morning we got up and took leave of those people.

On to greener pastures, as they say. It was down through Spokane and across Idaho then Montana and very soon we were racing the weather right along under the Canadian border through Columbus, Des Lacs, and then we were in Bottineau County and soon home. We'd made most of the trip, that summer, without putting up the car hood at all. We got home just in time, it turned out, for the army to remember Henry had signed up to join it.

I don't wonder that the army was so glad to get my brother that they turned him into a Marine. He was built like a brick outhouse anyway. We liked to tease him that they really wanted him for his Indian nose. He had a nose big and sharp as a hatchet, like the nose on Red Tomahawk, the Indian who killed Sitting Bull, whose profile is on signs all along the North Dakota highways. Henry went off to training camp, came home once during Christmas, then the next thing you know we got an overseas letter from him. It was 1970, and he said he was stationed up in the northern hill country. Whereabouts I did not know. He wasn't such a hot letter writer, and only got off two before the enemy caught him. I could never keep it straight, which direction those good Vietnam soldiers were from.

I wrote him back several times, even though I didn't know if those letters would get through. I kept him informed all about the car. Most of the time I had it up on blocks in the yard or half taken apart, because that long trip did a hard job on it under the hood.

I always had good luck with numbers, and never worried about the draft myself. I never even had to think about what my number

continued . . .

was. But Henry was never lucky in the same way as me. It was at least three years before Henry came home. By then I guess the whole war was solved in the government's mind, but for him it would keep on going. In those years I'd put his car into almost perfect shape. I always thought of it as his car while he was gone, even though when he left he said, "Now it's yours," and threw me his key.

"Thanks for the extra key," I'd said. "I'll put it up in your drawer just in case I need it." He laughed.

When he came home, though, Henry was very different, and I'll say this: the change was no good. You could hardly expect him to change for the better, I know. But he was quiet, so quiet, and never comfortable sitting still anywhere but always up and moving around. I thought back to times we'd sat still for whole afternoons, never moving a muscle, just shifting our weight along the ground, talking to whoever sat with us, watching things. He'd always had a joke, then, too, and now you couldn't get him to laugh, or when he did it was more the sound of a man choking, a sound that stopped up the throats of other people around him. They got to leaving him alone most of the time, and I didn't blame them. It was a fact: Henry was jumpy and mean.

I'd bought a color TV set for my mom and the rest of us while Henry was away. Money still came very easy. I was sorry I'd ever bought it though, because of Henry. I was also sorry I'd bought color, because with black-and-white the pictures seem older and farther away. But what are you going to do? He sat in front of it, watching it, and that was the only time he was completely still. But it was the kind of stillness that you see in a rabbit when it freezes and before it will bolt. He was not easy. He sat in his chair gripping the armrests with all his might, as if the chair itself was moving at a high speed and if he let go at all he would rocket forward and maybe crash right through the set.

Once I was in the room watching TV with Henry and I heard his teeth click at something. I looked over, and he'd bitten through his lip. Blood was going down his chin. I tell you right then I wanted to smash that tube to pieces. I went over to it but Henry must have known what I was up to. He rushed from his chair and shoved me out of the way, against the wall. I told myself he didn't know what he was doing.

My mom came in, turned the set off real quiet, and told us she had made something for supper. So we went and sat down. There was still blood going down Henry's chin, but he didn't notice it and no one said anything, even though every time he took a bite of his bread his blood fell onto it until he was eating his own blood mixed in with the food.

While Henry was not around we talked about what was going to happen to him. There were no Indian doctors on the reservation, and my mom was afraid of trusting Old Man Pillager because he courted her long ago and was jealous of her husbands. He might take revenge through her son. We were afraid that if we brought Henry to a regular hospital they would keep him.

"They don't fix them in those places," Mom said; "they just give them drugs."

"We wouldn't get him there in the first place," I agreed, "so let's just forget about it."

Then I thought about the car.

Henry had not even looked at the car since he'd gotten home, though like I said, it was in tip-top condition and ready to drive. I thought the car might bring the old Henry back somehow. So I bided my time and waited for my chance to interest him in the vehicle.

One night Henry was off somewhere. I took myself a hammer. I went out to that car and I did a number on its underside. Whacked it up. Bent the tail pipe double. Ripped the muffler loose. By the time I was done with the car it looked worse than any typical Indian car that has been driven all its life on reservation roads, which they always say are like government promises—full of holes. It just about hurt me, I'll tell you that! I threw dirt in the carburetor and I ripped all the electric tape off the seats. I made it look just as beat up as I could. Then I sat back and waited for Henry to find it.

Still, it took him over a month. That was all right, because it was just getting warm enough, not melting, but warm enough to work outside.

"Lyman," he says, walking in one day, "that red car looks like shit."

"Well it's old," I says. "You got to expect that."

"No way!" says Henry. "That car's a classic! But you went and ran the piss right out of it, Lyman, and you know it don't deserve that. I kept that car in A-one shape. You don't remember. You're too young. But when I left, that car was running like a watch. Now I don't even know if I can get it to start again, let alone get it anywhere near its old condition."

"Well you try," I said, like I was getting mad, "but I say it's a piece of junk."

Then I walked out before he could realize I knew he'd strung together more than six words at once.

continued . . .

After that I thought he'd freeze himself to death working on that car. He was out there all day, and at night he rigged up a little lamp, ran a cord out the window, and had himself some light to see by while he worked. He was better than he had been before, but that's still not saying much. It was easier for him to do the things the rest of us did. He ate more slowly and didn't jump up and down during the meal to get this or that or look out the window. I put my hand in the back of the TV set, I admit, and fiddled around with it good, so that it was almost impossible now to get a clear picture. He didn't look at it very often anyway. He was always out with that car or going off to get parts for it. By the time it was really melting outside, he had it fixed.

I had been feeling down in the dumps about Henry around this time. We had always been together before. Henry and Lyman. But he was such a loner now that I didn't know how to take it. So I jumped at the chance one day when Henry seemed friendly. It's not that he smiled or anything. He just said, "Let's take that old shitbox for a spin." Just the way he said it made me think he could be coming around.

We went out to the car. It was spring. The sun was shining very bright. My only sister, Bonita, who was just eleven years old, came out and made us stand together for a picture. Henry leaned his elbow on the red car's windshield, and he took his other arm and put it over my shoulder, very carefully, as though it was heavy for him to lift and he didn't want to bring the weight down all at once.

"Smile," Bonita said, and he did.

That picture. I never look at it anymore. A few months ago, I don't know why, I got his picture out and tacked it on the wall. I felt good about Henry at the time, close to him. I felt good having his picture on the wall, until one night when I was looking at television. I was a little drunk and stoned. I looked up at the wall and Henry was staring at me. I don't know what it was, but his smile had changed, or maybe it was gone. All I know is I couldn't stay in the same room with that picture. I was shaking. I got up, closed the door, and went into the kitchen. A little later my friend Ray came over and we both went back into that room. We put the picture in a brown bag, folded the bag over and over tightly, then put it way back in a closet.

I still see that picture now, as if it tugs at me, whenever I pass that closet door. The picture is very clear in my mind. It was so sunny that day Henry had to squint against the glare. Or maybe the camera Bonita held flashed like a mirror, blinding him, before she snapped the picture. My face is right out in the sun, big and round. But he might have drawn back, because the shadows on his face are deep as holes. There are two shadows curved like little hooks around the ends of his smile, as if to frame it and try to keep it there—that one, first smile that looked like it might have hurt his face. He has his field jacket on and the worn-in clothes he'd come back in and kept wearing ever since. After Bonita took the picture, she went into the house and we got into the car. There was a full cooler in the trunk. We started off, east, toward Pembina and the Red River because Henry said he wanted to see the high water.

The trip over there was beautiful. When everything starts changing, drying up, clearing off, you feel like your whole life is starting. Henry felt it, too. The top was down and the car hummed like a top. He'd really put it back in shape, even the tape on the seats was very carefully put down and glued back in layers. It's not that he smiled again or even joked, but his face looked to me as if it was clear, more peaceful. It looked as though he wasn't thinking of anything in particular except the bare fields and windbreaks and houses we were passing.

The river was high and full of winter trash when we got there. The sun was still out, but it was colder by the river. There were still little clumps of dirty snow here and there on the banks. The water hadn't gone over the banks yet, but it would, you could tell. It was just at its limit, hard swollen, glossy like an old gray scar. We made ourselves a fire, and we sat down and watched the current go. As I watched it I felt something squeezing inside me and tightening and trying to let go all at the same time. I knew I was not just feeling it myself; I knew I was feeling what Henry was going through at that moment. Except that I couldn't stand it, the closing and opening. I jumped to my feet. I took Henry by the shoulders and I started shaking him. "Wake up," I says, "wake up, wake up, wake up!" I didn't know what had come over me. I sat down beside him again.

His face was totally white and hard. Then it broke, like stones break all of a sudden when water boils up inside them.

"I know it," he says. "I know it. I can't help it. It's no use."

We start talking. He said he knew what I'd done with the car. It was obvious it had been whacked out of shape and not just neglected. He said he wanted to give the car to me for good now, it was no use. He said he'd fixed it just to give it back and I should take it.

"No way," I says, "I don't want it."

"That's okay," he says, "you take it."

"I don't want it, though," I says back to him, and then to emphasize, just to emphasize, you understand, I touch his shoulder. He slaps my hand off.

"Take that car," he says.

continued . . .

"No," I say, "make me," I say, and then he grabs my jacket and rips the arm loose. That jacket is a class act, suede with tags and zippers. I push Henry backwards, off the log. He jumps and bowls me over. We go down in a clinch and come up swinging hard, for all we're worth, with our fists. He socks my jaw so hard I feel like it swings loose. Then I'm at his ribcage and land a good one under his chin so his head snaps back. He's dazzled. He looks at me and I look at him and then his eyes are full of tears and blood and at first I think he's crying. But no, he's laughing. "Ha! Ha!" he says. "Ha! Ha! Take good care of it."

"Okay," I says, "okay, no problem. Ha! Ha!"

I can't help it, and I start laughing, too. My face feels fat and strange, and after a while I get a beer from the cooler in the trunk, and when I hand it to Henry he takes his shirt and wipes my germs off. "Hoof-and-mouth disease," he says. For some reason this cracks me up, and so we're really laughing for a while, and then we drink all the rest of the beers one by one and throw them in the river and see how far, how fast, the current takes them before they fill up and sink.

"You want to go on back?" I ask after a while. "Maybe we could snag a couple nice Kashpaw girls."

He says nothing. But I can tell his mood is turning again.

"They're all crazy, the girls up here, every damn one of them."

"You're crazy too," I say, to jolly him up. "Crazy Lamartine boys!"

He looks as though he will take this wrong at first. His face twists, then clears, and he jumps up on his feet. "That's right!" he says. "Crazier'n hell. Crazy Indians!"

I think it's the old Henry again. He throws off his jacket and starts swinging his legs out from the knees like a fancy dancer. He's down doing something between a grouse dance and a bunny hop, no kind of dance I ever saw before, but neither has anyone else on all this green growing earth. He's wild. He wants to pitch whoopee! He's up and at me and all over. All this time I'm laughing so hard, so hard my belly is getting tied up in a knot.

"Got to cool me off!" he shouts all of a sudden. Then he runs over to the river and jumps in.

There's boards and other things in the current. It's so high. No sound comes from the river after the splash he makes, so I run right over. I look around. It's getting dark. I see he's halfway across the water already, and I know he didn't swim there but the current took him. It's far. I hear his voice, though, very clearly across it.

"My boots are filling," he says.

He says this is in a normal voice, like he just noticed and he doesn't know what to think of it. Then he's gone. A branch comes by.

Another branch. And I go in.

By the time I get out of the river, off the snag I pulled myself onto, the sun is down. I walk back to the car, turn on the high beams, and drive it up the bank. I put it in first gear and then I take my foot off the clutch. I get out, close the door, and watch it plow softly into the water. The headlights reach in as they go down, searching, still lighted even after the water swirls over the back end. I wait. The wires short out. It is all finally dark. And then there is only the water, the sound of it going and running and going and running and running.

Louise Erdrich

Rancher

It was a place
with ashtrays
and adventure magazines
a spinout of smells
and coal oil

the kitchen was
for shaven men
cowboys
trying to rope life
or floral women

there were no
Stetsons
in the hat boxes

draped over
a civilized couch
some desperate clothes.

Life is delicate
in the city
compared to those funnel shapes
that did the hula
then jumped the state.

The others are
shadows in a tree line
shovelling mud,
frantic insects.
Good as watchdogs
They think like that.

Sid Larson

Minneapolis

Blackened trees
Limbless from industrial accidents
Huddle on the outskirts of the city.

The swamp has become a supermarket overnight.
A heron with no business sense
Vanishes.

The hungry man from the woods
Feeds on loose change
Like a parking meter.

At night
The smokestacks sink into the prairie.
Underground the soot changes hands.
The night shift moves slowly
Emitting a dim light from their mole eyes.

An odor of small lakes
Survives in the clothing of insects.

Tom Hennen

Eating the World

And this is the way you eat oatmeal.
And this is the blue china bowl
and the spoon with the rose in the handle.
And this is the mother who fills the bowl
with hot oatmeal, smooth as mud,
and sprinkles the sugar brown as sand
and pours the milk white as the new moon.
You make the main road first,
and it must split the middle
and then you wait
while the main road fills with milk
and melted sugar.

continued . . .

The next road crosses the main road
and it may bend if you want it to.
And it fills and so do the others.
You make a maze of milky roads.
And then you eat an empty lot,
and then a neighborhood.
Leave the farmland for last.
And this is the way you eat oatmeal
at my house.
And the mother is still there
and I am small, consuming my oatmeal world
to the bottom of the blue china bowl,
sucking the last drop of milk
from the spoon with the rose in the handle.

Nancy Veglahn

Looking at Models in the Sears Catalogue

These are our immortals.
They stand around
and always look happy.
Some must do work,

they are dressed for it,
but stay meticulously
clean. Others
play forever,
at the beach, in backyards,
but never move
strenuously. Here
the light is such
there are no shadows.
If anyone gestures,
it is with an open
hand. And the smiles
that bloom everywhere
are permanent, always
in fashion.

                           So
it is surprising to discover
children here,
who must have sprung
from the dark of some loins.
For the mild bodies
of these men and women
have learned to stay
dry and cool:
even the undressed
in bras and briefs
could be saying,
It was a wonderful dinner,
thank you so much.
                                  Yet,
season after season,
we shop here:
in Spring's pages,
no ripe abundance
overwhelms us;
in Winter's pages,
nothing is dying.
It is a kind of perfection.
We are not a people
who abide ugliness.
All the folds in the clothing
are neat folds,
nowhere to get lost.

                   Philip Dacey

Grazing Cattle

As we walk across the fields
they are lifting their
heads, lifting their slow
heads from grazing.
Forgetting the vegetable
kingdom of weeds and
grasses, the vegetable
kingdom of slow chewing.

continued . . .

From all this they are
lifting their heads,
all ten white-faced,
like things coming
up from vegetable sleep.
They watch us come closer,
the murk of their brown eyes
clearing to take us completely
in, like clumps of grass
pulled up all at once.
Poised, there is a clear
stillness of being awake.
We are images only in the
quiet kingdom of their eyes.
then their heads descend
in a row of slow motion to the
stomach sleep that we are not
part of. To a dream where we
don't belong.

Susan Strayer Deal

Hollyhocks

I

Fighting the tomatoes and sweet corn for light,
those wayward flowers clustered in my mother's garden.
Too stately for weeds, too plentiful
to be cherished, they spread in tight bunches,
nodding over the clothesline, peering in the kitchen.
They stuck close to the house, renewed each year
in the same places, safe from the plow,
safe from rooting hogs.
If their seeds wind-scattered beyond the hen house,
they tumbled unsprouted. Nothing lived easily
among the fireweed, the goldenrod
and the sharp rows of milo.

II

I stripped the showy spikes
and arranged my floral booty on the grass.
A toothpick jammed through the stem,
and each flower became a grand lady
draped in cloth of burgundy or scarlet.
Headless, flat-chested as I,
they glided in cotillions and quadrilles,
given grace by my hands.
But when I heard my father's tractor
and saw him driving up the pasture lane,
I left them motionless, dumb,
to run to the big wooden gate
and swing it open for him.
The discarded ladies lolled on the grass,
their flounces wrinkling into torn petals.

III

As he drove through the gate I held,
he looked straight ahead, and I swung behind him,
my greeting overcome by the machine's noise.
Mother's face pressed against the window, distorted
by the glass, and I knew just how she stood:
leaning forward, on one foot, hands braced on the sink.
The tractor sputtered out its hold on my father
and I watched his leg clear the seat
and touch him to the earth.
His face was caked with the gray soil he cultivated,
matching the evening drab of the farmyard,
the gravel, the silo and the elms indistinguishable
by color. With the strangling gray of dusk,
the hollyhocks were dull as pigweeds,
each bloom a faded trumpet, without sound.

Kathleene West

Swans

Cutting the swans free was the easy job. They all knew the storm was building. They could see it move, county to county, then reach the other side of the lake. She couldn't understand why she wasn't asked to take the laundry in, that was a hard job, strung on many white clotheslines, poles anchored on either side of the canal, clothes dancing like ghosts, barely reachable, as people leaned from either side of the water to pull them free into the baskets. The cabins on shore already looked restless, as if they wanted to blow away just from spite. The summer people were frightened but competent. When they told her to cut the swans free they gave her a hatchet. She preferred scissors, but there was not time and the rope was thick. The swans were tethered together, tied around their necks and then to each other. They were a group, not just three swans, or six, maybe nine or thirteen, and the rope, though fairly tied, would choke them if the wind threw them against the wall of any cabin. Cut free, they would bob together through the wild waves, tied to each other but not to the spike one of the summer visitors had hammered deep into the ground at the beginning of the season. The hatchet was easy to hold. She swung it once and the ends of the rope pulled apart from each other, swiftly unravelling until the ends were like horse's manes. The swans drifted away from shore. She watched them for a long time, riding the lake's waves like white messages someone had remembered to send to a lover after too much silence, after that time when certainty turns only to hope, but before the dull vacancy sets in and completes the absence. Cutting the swans free was the easy job, and the wind was exceptional, and she felt the shoreline wouldn't be complete without her standing there.

Deborah Keenan

Killing the Swallows

Dusk,
I sit with my brother
on a chair of baled straw
at the center of the haymow,
counting rocks.
We will divide the total
as carefully as if candling eggs,
then decide from whom, and from how many,
to draw the blood.

The rocks have come from the pasture,
from small knobs of ungrassed earth
washed clean by rain.
The swallows do not know this:
that with each rain
a fresh span of death
surfaces, then in the sunlight
fairly gleams.

Nor do they know that darkness
means more, perhaps, than a brief sleep.
Thus they dip their narrow wings,
as if layers of innocence,
into the haymow and
onto the topmost beam.

We sense more than see them,
my brother like a small towheaded priest
over his pyramid of stones,
I thumbing the switch
on the flashlight, waiting.
The birds, ignorant of rain and darkness,
know little more of light:
they disappear soft as down
into the struts and the rafters.
We will kill as many of them
as we have stomachs for,
and call it, if anything, man's need.

We will trust then to the cats
to do what remains
of the honors.

Thus we wait.
And the ritual occurs,
no more untoward than breathing.
The rock from the slingshot
follows its bright light upward,
finds its mark in the seed-heavy
belly of the bird.
Again and again the ritual occurs:
occurs the ritual, again and again and again,

continued . . .

sun rising, sun delivering,
sun going down.

In the gathering shadows
tribesmen touch their fingers
to spears honed bright
with spittle and flint.
They will depend upon
an ageless cluster of daughters,
the Pleiades, to cap their day.
They believe that man, more fortunate,
had been born in wraps of fur or feathers,
and they are far too lean,
and far too proud in blood,
ever to turn away.

William Kloefkorn

The Wrestle: From *Lord Grizzly*

"Whaugh!" A great belly grunt burped up from the white sands directly in front of him. And with a tremendous tumbler's heave of body, a silvertipped gray she-grizzly, *Ursus horribilis,* rose up before him on two legs. "Whaugh!" Two little brown grizzly cubs ducked cowering and whimpering behind the old lady.

The massive silvertipped beast came toward him, straddling, huge head dipped down at him from a humped neck, humped to strike him. Her big doglike mouth and piglike snout were bloody with chokecherry juice. Her long gray claws were bloody with fruit juice too. Her musky smell filled the air. And smelling the musk, Hugh knew then why Old Blue had bolted and run.

Hugh backed in terror, his heart suddenly burning hot and bounding around in his chest. The little arteries down his big Scotch nose wriggled red. His breath caught. The sense of things suddenly unraveling, of the end coming on, of being no longer in control of either things or his life, possessed him.

She was big as a great bull standing on two legs. She was so huge on her two legs that her incredible speed coming toward him actually seemed slow. Time stiffened, poured like cold molasses.

She roared. She straddled toward him on her two rear legs. She loomed over him, silver neck ruffed and humped, silver head pointed down at him. Her pink dugs stuck out at him. She stunk of dogmusk.

She hung over him, huge furry arms ready to cuff and strike. Her red-stained ivorygray claws, each a lickfinger long, each curved a little like a cripple's iron hook, closed and unclosed.

Hugh's eyes set; stiffened; yet he saw it all clearly. Time poured slow—yet was fast.

Hugh jerked up his rifle.

But the Old Lady's mammoth slowness was faster. She was upon him before he got his gun halfway up. She poured slow—yet was fast. "Whaugh!" She cuffed at the gun in his hands as if she knew what it was for. The gun sprang from his hands. As it whirled into the bushes, it went off in the air, the ball whacking harmlessly into the white sand at their feet.

Hugh next clawed for his horse pistol.

Again she seemed to know what it was for. She cuffed the pistol out of his hand too.

Hugh stumbled over a rock; fell back on his hands and rump;

continued . . .

like a tumbler bounded up again.

The cubs whimpered behind her.

The whimpering finally set her off. She struck. "Whaugh!" Her right paw cuffed him on the side of the head, across the ear and along the jaw, sending his wolfskin cap sailing, the claws ripping open his scalp. The blow knocked him completely off his feet, half-somersaulted him in the air before he hit ground.

Again, like a tumbler, Hugh bounded to his feet, ready for more. He felt very puny. The silvertip became a silver blur in his eyes. She became twice, thrice, magnified.

It couldn't be true, he thought. He, Old Hugh Glass, he about to be killed by a monster varmint? Never.

Hugh crouched over. He backed and filled downstream as best he could.

The she-grizzly, still on two legs, both paws ready to cuff, came after him, closed once more. She roared.

Hugh scratched for his skinning knife. There was nothing for it but to close with her. Even as her great claw swiped at him, stiff but swift, he leaped and got inside her reach. Her clubbing paw swung around him instead of catching him. He hugged her for dear life. He pushed his nose deep into her thick dogmusky whitegray fur. He pressed into her so hard one of her dugs squirted milk over his leathers.

She roared above him. She cuffed around him like a heavy-weight trying to give a lightweight a going-over in a clinch. She poured slow—yet was fast. She snarled; roared. His ear was tight on the huge barrel of her chest, and the roars reverberated inside her chest like mountain avalanches. He hugged her tight and stayed inside her reach. She clawed at him clumsily. Her ivorygray claws brought up scraps of buckskin shirt and strips of skin from his back.

He hugged her. And hugging her, at last got his knife around and set. He punched. His knife punged through the tough hide and slipped into her belly just below the ribs with an easy slishing motion. He stabbed again. Again and again. The knife punged through the tough furred hide each time and then slid in easy.

Blood spurted over his hands, over his belly, over his legs and her legs both, came in gouts of sparkling scarlet.

He wrestled her; stabbed her.

The great furred she-grizzly roared in an agony of pain and rage. He was still inside her reach and she couldn't get a good swipe at him. She clawed clumsily up and down his back. She brought up strips of leather and skin and red muscle. She pawed and clawed, until at last Hugh's ribs began to show white and clean.

Hugh screamed. He stabbed wildly, frantically, skinning knife sinking in again and again.

Her massive ruffed neck humped up in a striking curve. Then her head dug down at him. She seized his whole head in her red jaws and lifted him off his feet.

Hugh got in one more lunging thrust. His knife sank in all the way up to the haft directly over the heart.

He felt her dogteeth crunch into his skull. She shook him by the head like a dog might shake a doll. His body dangled. His neck cracked.

He screamed. His scream rose into a shrill squeak.

He sank away, half-conscious.

She dropped him.

Raging, blood spouting from a score of wounds, she picked him up again, this time by his game leg, and shook him violently, shook him until his leg popped in its hip socket. She roared while she gnawed. She was a great cat chewing and subduing a struggling mouse. His game leg cracked.

She dropped him.

Snarling, still spouting blood on all sides, coughing blood, she picked him up again, this time by the rump. She tore out a hunk the size of a buffalo boss and tossed it over her shoulder toward the brown cubs.

Hugh lay limp, sinking away. He thought of the boy Jim, of Bending Reed, of a picture-purty she-rip back in Lancaster, of two boy babies.

Time poured slow—yet space was quick.

The next thing he knew she had fallen on him and lay dead-heavy over his hips and legs.

He heard a scrambling in the brush. He heard the voices of men. He heard the grizzly cubs whimpering. He heard two shots.

Dark silence.

Frederick Manfred

Before Owls Sleep

The coyote stalks before owls sleep,
paws cleaving flowers
in frost, nose pleated
with essence of scouring calf
dehydrating in a week's wet.
I measure him with my bead.

Not hungry enough, he trots
the first field back to the river,
puffs of mud bouncing behind him
like short ghosts. Before disappearing
behind trees, he pauses,
turns to consider the feast.
In that revolution
I drop him with one squeeze.

Shirley Buettner

Coming Home,
Memorial Day, 1987

We brought mock orange and peach
colored roses in coffee cans
to Grandmother's and Grandfather's
graves, and my father glanced over
the field of cut stones and said,
"Ninety percent of the flowers here
today are plastic." I wasn't sure
how he meant it, until now, walking
in his pasture, coming upon this
winter-killed heifer, her empty grin,
and the Red Admiral in the rib cage,
opening and closing its stark wings.

Steven Hind

If I Ran the World

I will want first to free all
the animals in captivity. I will go
first to zoos, then to laboratories,
then to farms. From the zoo the lion
will wander stunned. The elephant will
grow thick fur in the northern winter.
The tiger will learn to hunt turkeys
and the cow and the python will
coil together. All the glossed over
eyes will open. I will clean the
dirt from the ears and shout into
them. I will say, go, make jungle.
The earth will be peopled again.

The zoo keepers I will absorb into
the growing industry of animal watching.
The little they know will come in handy
in telling a lion from a zebra. They
will come back from the edge of the forests
and tell me, the lions are on the increase,
the gorillas could be happier, the
buffalo have eaten all the grass
and they are stumped by tar. So I will be
able to issue orders to rip up the tar
and plant more buffalo grass.

Those animals that will want to come back
may come back. The cows can come back,
the barns will be standing still,
the horses can come back to the fields,
but there will be no more horse shows.
All the animals that are ready for slaughter
can be slaughtered.

Then I will ban the cars from the land.
We will cut their tops off and fill
them with dirt and plant beautiful flowers.

At first the animals will work themselves

continued . . .

deep into the woods to excape us, but as
we grow quieter and quieter, they will emerge.
Then we will look in their eyes and see ourselves,
and then the bars will begin to fall down
from around our own lives.

Greg Kuzma

Recovery

One day
I will look across
the plains of Stanley County

and the tractors will be gone

The barbed wire will
twist and dry into
the shape of snake skins
            and
all the herefords of the world
will be
grazing concrete east of Sioux Falls

By then   the land will be
wrinkled and stiff
as a dish rag
used and thrown away

            the antelope and grouse
a small dark clot on the brains
            of old men

Tourists
driving to see the uranium pits
and electric animals
of the Black Hills
            will not stray
from the highway

will now allow   their eyes
to notice
            the small bright shoots
of buffalo grass

beginning to breathe
                        in the ditch.

Kevin Woster

Letting the Wind Talk

Nature, the real world of physical cause and effect, is constant subject matter for most of the contemporary writers of this area. But writers of all times and places have turned frequently to nature for content. Why?

One reason is, writers are attracted to and energized by extremes, and in nature there is often muscular intensity, things absolutely wild which contrast dramatically with sedate civilization. Things which command attention. Living in genteel England, the poet William Blake saw deeply into the jungle dark in his "The Tyger", and what he saw led him to intense questions:

> *Tyger! Tyger! burning bright*
> *In the forests of the night,*
> *What immortal hand or eye*
> *Could frame thy fearful symmetry?*
>
> *In what distant deeps or skies*
> *Burnt the fire of thine eyes?*
> *On what wings dare he aspire?*
> *What the hand, dare seize the fire?*

Blake's beast is never found in cages at zoos. What's there is living taxidermy, sofa pillow non-beasts sprawled out on hot concrete. Tigers are in the jungle, wild opposites of what we usually experience, moving with irresistible grace and power, fascinating in their fierce difference. Later in his poem, moved to awe by what he imagined, Blake asked ultimate questions about the amazing diversity of nature:

> *When the stars threw down their spears,*
> *And water'd heaven with their tears,*
> *Did he smile his work to see?*
> *Did he who made the Lamb make thee?*

These and Blake's other questions apply well to the natural intensities found throughout this section: wolves, the wind, coyotes, nighthawks, lightning, hunting owls, fire, a screaming bluejay, the eternal rock, rain, migrating geese, aged trees. These are examples of nature being absolutely itself, demanding to be considered.

And when nature is most fully itself, it is creatively mysterious, and naturally provokes questions. Like Blake and others, the writers of this area interrogate the creative unknowns of nature. They imaginatively examine what remains of the wild world around them. In works like "South Dakota Night," "Hunting Pheasants in a Cornfield," "Passing On Through Faith," and "Smoke", these writers are stirred by what is just beyond the rim of what they too easily experience and define. Mystery is infinite possibility.

But "out there" is not the only mystery. Writers can be equally inspired by a close examination of the near things of their place. They can, as Blake once said, "see the world in a grain of sand." In this section, there are also many explorations of the mysteries and potential meanings of small particulars, many celebrations of what the author of "Porch Swing in September" calls "one world at a time." He presents the environment of his "small brown spider" in exquisite detail. Similarly, the novelist Frederick Manfred and the authors of "Staying in One Place", "Baltimore Oriole", "A Burial, Green", "Cardinal Rules," "Three Kinds of Pleasures," and "Horizontal Grandeur" describe specifics which are almost endlessly informative. In the latter work, the author echoes Blake when he says "a prairie man looks at a square foot and he sees a whole universe."

It's possible, of course, to look so *exclusively* that only one thing is seen. The microscopic eye can reduce us if it narrows our vision. But artists usually see more broadly as they look closely, because they connect what they see with other things. These people see physical connections, and they also see the connections we call metaphors. Writers, especially, are inclined to see metaphorical relationships, relationships on the level of meaning, between things which at first seem completely unlike each other. Some of these writers see so many relationships that they become convinced of the essential unity of all things.

There are many such writers in our midwestern region, and many examples of that bifocal artistic vision in this section. For instance, in "Now I Know Grouse," "The Rock," "The Cottonwood," "Approaching Winter,"and "Echo," there are powerful progressions from specific physical circumstances to wider world contemplations, questions, conclusions. The physical beginnings of each of these works are originative. They are blood and bone realities out of which meanings evolve.

But not in any linear sense. These works are not philosophical progressions out of and away from the natural world. They are not modern movements from the concrete to the cerebral. Rather, they are circles, meditations which bomerang back to intensify the physical identities of the writers who have created them. These writings and the others in this section are dramatic proofs of the best that nature can be for us: a reminder of our physical origins and evidence of the physical beings that we are. Through nature, these writers suggest, we can sharpen and learn to trust our instincts, be comforted by natural process, know that we are not alone or estranged but connected, and sense and take our places in the world.   We can be like the Chippewa singer of this dream song:

> *as my eyes*
> *search*
> *the prairie*
> *I feel the summer*
> *in the spring*

Finally, we can even regain what the writer of "Letting The Wind Talk" calls "the old feeling," through listening to and understanding "the prairie wind and the call of the migrating geese over the melting snow."   Through realizing the natural world, all of this section's writers suggest to us, we can realize our natural, physical, multi-sensory selves.   We can be at home in our world.

South Dakota Night

At midnight in midwinter the sky is a deep blue-black, lit only by a few cold stars and shards of ice in the deepest ruts. The temperature reached nearly fifty today, and the scent from the deep golden grasses on the rolling hills south of the house hangs in the air, tangy and sweet, mixed with the sharper odor of manure from the corrals, and the heavy scent of burning wood. Moonlight gives a faint silver sheen to tall bronze bluestem, tawny foxtail, brown alfalfa.

I turn slowly, enjoying a skyline shaped by the smooth shapes of hills; no straight-sided buildings break that gentle arch, no trees slash upward. This is the prairie, during the annual warm spell between the first snow and the spring storms that strike when our cows begin calving in March. To the north, a glow marks the nearest town, twenty miles away. If I lean forward over the porch railing, I can see my neighbor's yard light a mile away.

As a city child, I lived in terror of the dark. Even now, on brief city visits, I lock doors and look wistfully out high windows at night, awakened by sirens and inexplicable shrieks. Out here, where strange sounds in the night may mean a prairie fire or someone stealing cows, I can't avoid the responsibility of investigating. But here the night is more than peaceful; it is inviting, an opportunity not to be missed. Often, I get up and prowl outside in my nightgown just for the pleasure of it.

On a moonless night when I was a teenager, I found myself on a tired horse far from home after dark. Coyotes howled; a booming rush overhead told me the nighthawks were hunting insects. In my fear, I complained to my horse, who blew her warm breath on my face and reminded me a good horse will take a rider home even in a blizzard. I mounted, loosened the reins, and waited. She raised her head and began trotting confidently straight into smothering blackness, as if a sack had dropped over my head. But I trusted her. Soon the nighthawks swirling around me became benevolent night spirits; the coyotes sounded happy to be alive. Grass swished against my horse's legs just as it did in daylight; my saddle squeaked. After awhile, I could see the birds, and the grass seemed to glow faintly, as if lit from within. Before I'd seen enough, I was home. My fear was gone.

A coyote howls from the east, near the carcass of a cow that died of old age yesterday. In the distance a series of puppy-like yips and yaps begin, and I can trace the young coyotes' high-spirited progress through the gully toward the dead cow by their cheerful arguing. If I wanted to leave the porch and walk a half- mile to the hilltop, I could hear them growling over the old cow's thin ribs. The cow had borne calves for us for almost twenty years, until her hips grated and rattled from the strain of her age. We thanked her as we dragged her to the pile of ancestral bones.

Directly below me, tall weeds around a waterhole rattle briefly—a coyote hunting mice, or a skunk headed for the compost, or the seven deer come for water. A yearling calf bawls, one of the bunch of twenty-six heifers we're raising for replacement breeding cows. They've been fed together since they were weaned and always move—like teenagers—in a compact and usually raucous bunch. Faintly I can see black shapes lying close together a half-mile away, and a light-colored blotch moving toward them from a gully. Perhaps they left her while she napped, and she woke alone, frightened as a child.

I inhale deeply, glad the blizzard roared over our heads two days ago. We could almost inhale snow from the heavy gray clouds, and the winds left a fifteen-foot hole in the plank corral, plastic flapping on barbed wire, hamburger cartons jammed under tumbleweeds in fence corners. The next blizzard is on its way, and we may not get off so lightly next time. When snow is piled deep on the plains, so even normal sounds are muffled, I put on my sheepskin moccasins before my midnight trips. But I still go.

If I'm patient, on some night when the thermometer reads ten or fifteen degrees below zero, I will hear the grouse calling. First a single note, like the mellow tone of a monastery bell, will ring from the top of a haystack, and be answered from the shelter of the willows down the gully. I'll try to get outside without making a sound. If I shut a door too hard, or speak, or even shiver, they stop and may not start again that night.

But if I am quiet enough, I might listen to them ringing back and forth across the prairie for an hour. Finally, with a thoroughly undignified squawk, the first one will launch itself awkwardly and fly toward the others. Then they will all take off, floundering in the air like flying turtles, clucking and muttering, until they bury themselves under a rosebush to peck after seeds and gossip for the rest of the night.

Then I move, take a step and hear the snow squeal with cold underfoot. Each step seems to reverberate until I can hear nothing else. The world shrinks to the sound of my footsteps—painfully symbolic—until I stop, and wait for the natural sounds to reassert themselves.

The neighbor's dog barks, a high, frantic yelping. The spell of the moonlight is broken. I'll come back another night, after the snow, to hear the grouse. Now it's time to go back to bed, the warm tangle of husband, dog and cat, to drift back to sleep among faint coyote howls.

Linda Hasselstrom

The Bare Facts

The spirit lives
when it moves and sings your name
when grandfather and coyote keep warm
together, and lizard gets damp
from the earth, stays fast and hard to kill,
when lark flies straight and high to clouds
and you see the buzzard weeping under blankets,
when butterfly still talks to women,
when ants still fight and die to carry stones,
seed-like and shiny, from mound to rattle,
when we hang by fingernails, remote and hidden,
at the ridge of words.

The end comes quick
when cricket tells us everything
he knows.

Elizabeth Cook-Lynn

Hunting Pheasants in a Cornfield

I

What is so strange about a tree alone in an open field?
It is a willow tree. I walk around and around it.
The body is strangely torn, and cannot leave it.
At last I sit down beneath it.

II

It is a willow tree alone in acres of dry corn.
Its leaves are scattered around its trunk, and around me,
Brown now, and speckled with delicate black.
Only the cornstalks now can make a noise.

III

The sun is cold, burning through the frosty distances of space.
The weeds are frozen to death long ago.
Why then do I love to watch
The sun moving on the chill skin of the branches?

IV

The mind has shed leaves alone for years.
It stands apart with small creatures near its roots.
I am happy in this ancient place,
A spot easily caught sight of above the corn,
If I were a young animal ready to turn home at dusk.

Robert Bly

Passing On Through Faith

Scurrying across the north-south highway
desperate whispers of ghosts
disperse in a swirl of snow. A few gray birds
peck away at the roadkill—then veer off
like a pale hand waving
from the first pickup that's come along
for miles and miles. Across the numb plain
the rumps of black angus are fleeced white.

Just outside Faith the graveyard bares
its bleak hill to the boring wind. The crucifixion
carved in marble hangs heavy
over the stones, heavy as the heart
in the throat the days they bury. Some dumb hawk
in the town tavern is always ready
to take off. Its stiff wings, spread
high over the heads at the bar, are covered
with dust. Somewhere out in the field deep mud
is slowly seeping up through hollow bones. The wind drones
"Fly home, fly home . . ." Seeking the dark
wet below, dreams float
down to earth like white feathers
of the snowstorm passing on
through Faith, South Dakota tonight.

Gary David

Smoke

Beyond the twirling keys of sycamores
and coil of anaconda hills,
smoke interrogates
a washed West Kansas sky.
As keen as cold
that tumbleweeds through trees,
white and icarian in a weight
of air, it soon convolves
and rises into space.

Not even a thrush
forgets itself to music
the way that silent smoke
involves itself in air.
Earth's own amplexity,
fat and fleshed and veined,
boned, limbed and skinned,
it grows somehow immune
to faltering or falling.

Evolving in a helicline
smoke commits itself
to constant reformation,
sometimes by drift of wind,
by sunlight and shade, humidity
and heat: existing
sometimes *no* and sometimes *yes*,
lost in a soul of sky,
inessential and complete.

Bruce Cutler

Porch Swing in September

The porch swing hangs fixed in a morning sun
that bleaches its gray slats, its flowered cushion
whose flowers have faded, like those of summer,
and a small brown spider has hung out her web
on a line between porch post and chain
so that no one may swing without breaking it.
She is saying it's time that the swinging were done with,
time that the creaking and pinging and popping
that sang through the ceiling were past,
time now for the soft vibrations of moths,
the wasp tapping each board for an entrance,
the cool dewdrops to brush from her work
every morning, one world at a time.

Ted Kooser

Blizzard

On the highway
herded by the wind
cars plow home.

There is no room
for sky or air
the space is filled
with white wings
that beat in thickest
rhythm
soundless and falling.

All night
I will dream of moths
and white birds.

Barbara Esbensen

All Souls

All day long the wind
pushes through cottonwoods
like the ghost of the sea.

> *May the pioneer women*
> *pray for us.*

> *May the Kansa*
> *the Pawnee*
> *and the Kiowa*
> *pray for us.*

> *May the wolves*
> *and the buffalo*
> *pray for us.*

Outside the window
a cherry tree stands
like a pale candle
burning in the rain.

Victor Contoski

From *Conquering Horse*

They saw him before he saw them. Omaha. They who went against the current.

There were four of them, three grown men and a youth. They were naked except for clout and moccasins, their faces fierce with war paint, their hair done up for action. They were looking directly at him. Then, casually, almost lazily, the tallest Omaha drew an arrow from his quiver and fitted it to his bow and let fly. The arrow came at him with a rush, enlarging, feather streaming, and then, *whinn*, missed him and fell slithering through the cattails behind him.

He dropped flat on his belly. His heart began to jump like a jackrabbit. "Now I will die in a strange place," he thought, "and my mother will never know where my bones lie drying. I will be one of those who went away alone and never returned."

He remembered the bravery of his father and got a grip on himself. If he was to die he had better die a brave man. The four Omaha were sure to boast of having killed him, a chief's son, and if he let them see he was afraid, word of it was bound to get back to his father.

He turned on his back and looked up at the cattails nodding above him. It occurred to him there had been no redwings hopping about in the cattails. "Ahh, the swamps are always full of happy redwings. I did not see that they had hidden themselves to warn me. My eyes were blind with foolishness."

He couldn't crawl because the Omaha were sure to see where the rushes stirred. He waited.

And waiting, his eye caught a quick, stealthy darting movement nearby, almost in his face. Focusing his eyes, close up, he saw a deer fly circling around and around the tip of his bow. The bow had his smell and the deer fly circled it. There was another stealthy whisk of movement off to one side and then he saw what had really caught his eye: a squat black spider with a yellow dot on its back. It was quickly weaving a web in the path of the circling deer fly, from one cattail stalk to another. He watched amazed as it shuttled back and forth. Line after line of glistening gossamer issued from its tail. Swiftly the net spread between the two cattails.

"It is a sign," he whispered. "If the black spider catches the fly, the Omaha will catch me. If she does not, they will miss me."

He heard the Omaha approaching. Their feet slid through the wet rushes, lifting out of reluctant mud. He guessed they were wading

continued . . .

abreast, coming straight for him, combing the narrow patch of cattails. He watched the spider and the circling deer fly at the same time that he listened for the Omaha.

They were almost on him. He was sure that they had already seen him. Yet the deer fly kept circling, circling, each time just barely missing the spider's web.

A foot landed almost in his face. It sank splashing in the mud immediately under his ear. Yet still the deer fly flew around and around.

He held his breath, eyes half closing.

The black spider flung one more strand. The deer fly hit it, stuck on it, buzzed fiercely a second, then broke free and flew off.

"Ai! they will miss me."

The next foot came down near his hip, again sinking some in the slime. It lifted slowly with a sucking sound; went on. He was safe. "Ae, I will still be known and return in safety to my mother's pot."

He lay a long time in the same position, waiting for the Omaha to leave the valley.

And waiting, he noticed that the spider's web had a diamond shape. The diamond shape reminded him of a story his father Redbird told. Returning from a hunt, young Redbird had become tired as night came on. Young Redbird had failed to get meat, or make a coup, and was sad about it. So young Redbird lay down in the deep grass on the open prairie and fell asleep. Awakening in the morning, his eyes opened on a spider web woven just above his nose in the tall grass. He looked at it a while. Dew drops glistened on the web in the clear morning light. Marveling at its great beauty, at its neat diamond design, he drifted off to sleep again. And dreamed of the diamond design. A voice told him to use it. The diamond pattern would bring luck to his tribe. When he returned home he told his father Wondering Man about the dream, about the voice, and Wondering Man, overjoyed that his son had returned safe, and full of reverent awe, told the people. Soon everyone was using the diamond pattern in their quillwork.

The cattails whispered overhead, roughly, then softly. No Name's heavy body pressed down into the undergrowth. Soft mud slowly welled between his shoulders. The damp cold came through his buckskins.

Thinking of his own carelessness in being caught by the Omahas, he remembered the story of another foolish youth, named Spider. Spider was out exploring one day and ran across some ripe chokecherries. Spider began stuffing himself with them, until his lips and tongue turned black and his throat almost puckered shut. At last the chokecherry tree decided Spider was making a pig of himself, so she whispered, "Little nephew, do not eat too much of me or your bowels will bind." This made Spider laugh. "Oh, that's all right, little mother tree. I've just had a lot of artichokes and they'll keep me loose." But his bowels did bind, and a few days later he was seen sitting on a hill facing the wind, trying, trying. Suddenly a rabbit ran between his legs. Astounded, he thought he had given birth to a son. Grabbing his clout, he jumped up and ran after it, calling, calling. "My son, my son, wait for me. I'm your father." But the rabbit got away. Muttering, cursing the bad manners of the new generation, Spider went back to his hill and sat down again. Except that this time he wrapped a robe around his legs and seat to make sure nothing could get away. At last it came. He folded his robe carefully over it, then quickly got a stick and began to pound it, crying, "Try to get away from me now, will you? My son you are and my son you will remain."

Thinking about the story again, No Name laughed merrily to himself.

The sun began to shine directly down upon him. It became sticky hot. A few mosquitoes got wind of him and despite the bright sun wisped out of the shadowy undergrowth and sat on him.

"Ae, they have come to tell me something. Perhaps the Omaha have gone."

He reset his wolf cap, then got up on hands and knees and like a skulking fourlegged peered through the cattails to all sides. The Omaha had left. Also, the swamp was suddenly full of singing redwings.

Frederick Manfred

Staying In One Place

Riding fence last summer
I saw a meadowlark caught by one wing.
(My father saw one caught so, once;
in freeing it, taught me compassion.)
                              He'd flown
futile circles around the wire, snapping bones.
Head folded on yellow breast,
he hung by one sinew, dead.

Gathering cattle in the fall
I rode that way again;
his yellow breast was bright as autumn air
or his own song.

I'm snowed in now, only a path
from the house to the cows in the corral.
Miles away he still hangs,
frost in his eyesockets,
swinging in the wind.

I lie heavy in my bed alone, turning turning,
seeing the house layered in drifts of snow
and dust and years and scraps of empty paper.
He should be light, light
bone and snowflake light.

                              Linda Hasselstrom

Winter Tree

This winter tree at
creekside is white
as the snow it digs its
roots into.
Split in the middle and
barkless on one side,
this old elm has come to
be known as the tree
that won't die, in spite
of what it's been through.
It's gnarled as a tree on
the moon might be.
One must look close
to find its shadow—the
shadow is frozen on the
snow, dark where it lies,
as if it melted its shape
there in a private rage.
Somewhere in its old
knotted heart is
greenwood that will
grow again in spring—
what winter could not
steal, what lightning did
not strike.

Nancy Peters Hastings

Funeral at Ansley

I write of a cemetery,
of the perpetual care of buffalo grass,
of kingbirds and catbirds
and cottonwoods;

of wild roses around headstones,
with their high thin stems
and their tight tines
and their blooms pursed
in the morning.

I write of old faces,
of cotton hose and flowered dresses
and mouths which have grown up
on the weather.

And I write of one woman
who lies a last time in the long sun
of August, uncramped by the wind
which autumns each one of us

under catbirds and kingbirds
and cottonwoods, and the gray-green
leaves of the buffalo grass.

Baltimore Oriole

This morning the oriole
is a good carpenter,
working itself
for the sake of its nest.

Hounding the right bits of grass,
it has turned flight
into a muscular blossoming.

The air is something
it keeps slipping into,
it is what it beats

into breath with its life.

Tonight the sky will be hung
with migrational stars,
it will be the dark hunting
ground of owls, the briefer tomb
of anything sleeping.

But tomorrow the oriole
will be at its work again,
and it will be singing.

Don Welch

A Burial, Green

It was afternoon, and my brother split
a turtle's head
open in the rain; the tiny skull
glistened, and soon the ants knew
every detail of cracked shell.
For hours he sat in the blue shade
of the elm, planning a burial
for his small dead, until
the shadows knew each curve
of grass around the green and orange
spotted shell, a tiny helmet
filling with air. It was spring
and the bark on the dogwood trees
was slick and wet, the cardinals twittered
on the green feeder.
And my brother thought it was ceremony,
the way the door to our white house opened
and he entered, done with his spade
and boots, the way my mother
hovered in the doorway
and touched his shoulder
without a word
like the rain.

Marcia Southwick

Dirt Farmer

I am a dirt farmer
Who dreams of poetry.
Is that so strange? Is anything?
I have bent myself thankfully
Over the heat of cowchips.
When the lespedeza flowers
I breathe its blooms.
The calf I winch to birth
Cows legs like oaks to graze on,
And stuck hogs bleed for breakfasts.
This morning at milking
I kissed the cow's warm flank
And she kicked the milk to froth beneath my knees.
I forgave her,
Then cried with the cats.
Now the manure is in bloom,
Thistles defend the driveway,
And corncobs gird the mud beneath my boots.
Plotting harvests,
I roam my acreage like a sweet spy.

William Kloefkorn

Cardinal Rules

nourish yourself
close to the ground
but when you fly
redden the sky with bright wings

stay close
to the cover of dark branches
a red
alert to danger
but not afraid

feed peacefully
with small chickadees and sparrows
content with crumbs
the world provides
enough

when the jay comes
hungry and screaming
vanish
like a flame
extinguished in the wind

and in the cold
in the days of iron frost
do not complain
but stuff your belly with the seeds
of your own burning
life
and fluff up your feathers
to hold in heat

even with your thin feet
deep in snow

sing

Nancy Paddock

Three Kinds of Pleasures

I

Sometimes, riding in a car, in Wisconsin
Or Illinois, you notice those dark telephone poles
One by one lift themselves out of the fence line
And slowly leap on the gray sky—
And past them, the snowy fields.

II

The darkness drifts down like snow on the picked cornfields
In Wisconsin: and on these black trees
Scattered, one by one,
Through the winter fields—
We see stiff weeds and brownish stubble,
And white snow left now only in the wheelruts of the
        combine.

III

It is a pleasure, also, to be driving
Toward Chicago, near dark,
And see the lights in the barns.
The bare trees more dignified than ever,
Like a fierce man on his deathbed,
and the ditches along the road half full of a private snow.

                                        Robert Bly

Horizontal Grandeur

For years I carried on a not-so-jovial argument with several friends who are north-woods types. They carted me out into the forests of northern Wisconsin or Minnesota, expected me to exclaim enthusiastically on the splendid landscape. "Looks fine," I'd say, "but there's too damn many trees, and they're all alike. If they'd cut down twenty miles or so on either side of the road, the flowers could grow, you could see the sky, and find out what the real scenery is like." Invariably, this provoked groans of disbelief that anyone could be insensitive enough to prefer dry, harsh, treeless prairies. There, a man is the tallest thing for miles around; a few lonesome cottonwoods stand with leaves shivering by a muddy creek; sky is large and readable as a Bible for the blind. The old farmers say you can see weather coming at you, not like woods, where it sneaks up and takes you by surprise.

I was raised in Minneota, true prairie country. When settlers arrived in the 1870's they found waist-high grass studded with wild flowers; the only trees were wavy lines of cottonwoods and willows along the crooked Yellow Medicine Creek. Farmers emigrated here not for scenery, but for topsoil; 160 flat acres without trees or boulders to break plows and cramp fields was beautiful to them. They left Norway, with its picturesque but small, poor, steep farms; or Iceland, where the beautiful backyard mountains frequently covered hay fields with lava and volcanic ash. Wives, described by Ole Rolvaag in *Giants in the Earth*, were not enamored with the beauty of black topsoil, and frequently went insane from loneliness, finding nowhere to hide on these blizzardy plains. But the beauty of this landscape existed in function, rather than form, not only for immigrant farmers, but for Indians who preceded them.

Blackfeet Indians live on the Rocky Mountains' east edge in northern Montana—next to Glacier National Park. Plains were home for men and buffalo, the source of Blackfeet life; mountains were for feasting and dancing, sacred visions and ceremonies, but home only for spirits and outlaws. It puzzles tourists winding up hairpin turns, looking down three thousand feet into dense forests on the McDonald Valley floor, that Blackfeet never lived there. It did not puzzle the old farmer from Minneota who, after living and farming on prairies most of his life, vacationed in the Rockies with his children after he retired. When they reached the big stone escarpment sticking up at the prairie's edge, one of his sons asked him how he liked the view. "These are

continued . . .

stone," the old man said; "I have stones in the north eighty. These are bigger, and harder to plow around. Let's go home."

When my mother saw the Atlantic Ocean in Virginia, she commented that though saltier, noiser, and probably somewhat larger, it was no wetter or more picturesque than Dead Coon Lake or the Yellow Medicine River and surely a good deal more trouble to cross.

There are two eyes in the human head—the eye of mystery, and the eye of harsh truth—the hidden and the open—the woods eye and the prairie eye. The prairie eye looks for distance, clarity, and light; the woods eye for closeness, complexity, and darkness. The prairie eye looks for usefulness and plainness in art and architecture; the woods eye for the baroque and ornamental. Dark old brownstones on Summit Avenue were created by a woods eye; the square white farmhouse and red barn are prairie eye's work. Sherwood Anderson wrote his stories with a prairie eye, plain and awkward, told in the voice of a man almost embarrassed to be telling them, but bullheadedly persistent to get at the meaning of the events; Faulkner, whose endless complications of motive and language take the reader miles behind the simple facts of an event, sees the world with a woods eye. One eye is not superior to the other, but they are different. To some degree, like male and female, darkness and light, they exist in all human heads, but one or the other seems dominant. The Manicheans were not entirely wrong.

I have a prairie eye. Dense woods or mountain valleys make me nervous. After once visiting Burntside Lake north of Ely for a week, I felt a fierce longing to be out. Driving home in the middle of the night, I stopped the car south of Willmar, when woods finally fell away and plains opened up. It was a clear night, lit by a brilliant moon turning blowing grasses silver. I saw for miles—endless strings of yardlights, stars fallen into the grovetops. Alone, I began singing at the top of my voice. I hope neither neighborhood cows, nor the Kandiyohi County sheriff were disturbed by this unseemly behavior from a grown man. It was simply cataracts removed from the prairie eye with a joyful rush.

Keep two facts in mind if you do not have a prairie eye: magnitude and delicacy. The prairie is endless! After the South Dakota border, it goes west for over a thousand miles, flat, dry, empty, lit by brilliant sunsets and geometric beauty. Prairies, like mountains, stagger the imagination most not in detail, but size. As a mountain is high, a prairie is wide; horizontal grandeur, not vertical. People neglect prairies as scenery because they require time and patience to comprehend. You eye a mountain, even a range, at a glance. The ocean spits and foams as its edge. You see down into the Grand Canyon. But walking the whole prairie might require months. Even in a car at 60 miles an hour it takes three days or more. Like a long symphony by Bruckner or

Mahler, prairie unfolds gradually, reveals itself a mile at a time, and only when you finish crossing it do you have any idea of what you've seen. Americans don't like prairies as scenery or for national parks and preserves because they require patience and effort. We want instant gratification in scenic splendor as in most things, and simply will not look at them seriously. Prairies are to Rockies what *Paradise Lost* is to haiku. Milton is cumulative; so are prairies. Bored for days, you are suddenly struck by the magnitude of what has been working on you. It's something like knowing a woman for years before realizing that you are in love with her after all.

If prairie size moves the imagination, delicacy moves the heart. West of Minneota, the prairies quickly rise several hundred feet and form the Coteau. This land looks more like the high plains of Wyoming. Rougher and stonier than land to the east, many sections have never been plowed. Past Hendricks, along the south and west lake shores, things open up—treeless hills with grazing cattle, gullies with a few trees sliding off toward the lake. Ditches and hillsides are a jumble of flowers, grasses and thistles: purple, pink, white, yellow, blue. In deep woods, the eye misses these incredible delicate colors, washed in light and shadow by an oversized sky. In the monochromatic woods, light comes squiggling through onto a black green shadowy forest floor. My eye longs for a rose, even a sow thistle.

A woods man looks at twenty miles of prairie and sees nothing but grass, but a prairie man looks at a square foot and sees a universe; ten or twenty flowers and grasses, heights, heads, colors, shades, configurations, bearded, rough, smooth, simple, elegant. When a cloud passes over the sun, colors shift, like a child's kaleidoscope.

I stop by a roadside west of Hendricks, walk into the ditch, pick a prairie rose. This wild pink rose is far lovelier than hot-house roses wrapped in crinkly paper that teenagers buy prom dates. The dusty car fills with its smell. I ignore it for a few minutes, go on talking. When I look again, it's dry, as if pressed in an immigrant Bible for a hundred years. These prairie flowers die quickly when you take them out of their own ground. They too are immigrants who can't transplant, and wither fast in their new world.

I didn't always love prairies. On my father's farm I dreamed of traveling, living by the sea and, most of all, close to mountains. As a boy, I lay head on a stone in the cow pasture east of the house, looking up at cloud rows in the west, imagining I saw all the way to the Rockies and that white tips on the clouds were snow on mountaintops or, better yet, white hair on sleeping blue elephant spines. Living in a flat landscape

continued . . .

drove me to indulge in mountainous metaphor, then later discover that reality lived up to it. When I finally saw the Rockies years later, they looked like pasture clouds, phantasmagorias solider than stone.

The most astonished travelers do not come from the Swiss Alps, or the California coast. Only William Carlos Williams, who lived in the industrial prairies of New Jersey, would notice the Mexico of *Desert Music*. A southwest poet with a wood's eye would have seen sequaro cactus or medieval parapets. Trust a prairie eye to find beauty and understate it truthfully, no matter how violent the apparent exaggeration. Thoreau, though a woodsman, said it right: "I can never exaggerate enough."

Bill Holm

Early Snow

Yesterday's maple
was a tipsy gypsy
tossing gifts
to the wind and the sun;
today he's caught
in white feather weather,
stealing chickens,
and he cannot run.

Carlee Swann

Line Storm

Only the wind is moving now, the grass
                turning in upon itself.
The farmer's boots stand empty on the porch.
Even the windows sleep.

Suddenly the eyes of the clouds are open,
the lightning stalks the windrows five miles down,
                closer and closer . . .

Out in the fields, all the
abandoned machines begin to awaken—
cornpickers, combines, balers
circling in a heavy dance,
rooting the ground with their snouts.
An ancient John Deere tractor is leading them . . .
westward, toward the conspiracy of clouds,
                the iron voices of the lightning.

And now they are waiting:
steaming and shuddering in the first assault of rain.

Mark Vinz

Field Work

On his last swing around
what I saw was the smoke
stack of his tractor, his head
rising over a sloped field,
the sun around, his body
flexed above the plow, pulling
open the ground for
whatever rain or sun was
coming to him.

He went down that way—
one leg dangling;
tripped up his plow and drove
through the west fence gate standing up

—into the clutter of his farmyard;
shut up the hogs; had a second thought:
dropped a tin can over the smoke stack.

                                    Doug Cockrell

Vagrants

Near the tag-end
of the glory days of the hobo
my brother and I took charge
of garden enough to keep
two boys in weeds a month of summers.
Beans, lettuce, radishes and
an acre and a half of potatoes lined rows
that narrowed in the distance
like railroad tracks. We kept one eye
on the road. Hoboes
would work for a meal.

Stooped, shuffling, hollow-eyed,
pants and shirt flapping in the hot wind
across a clotheshorse body,
he came to the back door.
Dad would say he'd been in jail,
the cops had used a hose on him.

Mom told him he didn't have to work.
"No, ma'am. I can't eat if I ain't worked."

We watched his hands crawl the rows,
knees and toes defining progress
slow as new roads across
unmapped prairie. One bean row
one gust of wind lifted
his shirttail off a lattice-work
of new scars. He more careful than the wind
lifted each hanging plant to
gently pull the young foxtail.

Mom would tell him enough,
he would thank her and
shuffle toward the railroad.
Where he left off
we'd scowl up the rows,
enthusiastic as yardbirds
eyeing a lifetime of rockpile.
A steam whistle would signal
drive wheels dragging west
a mile of empty boxcars.

Larry Holland

The Photographer

In the ditches beside the road
last year's empty milkweed pods
are standing in water. They would
like to grow again, to spit fine
silk into the wind. They can only
gape their winter blackened mouths
against the gray clouds of March.
These brittle shells will not soften.
I take their very last picture.

John R. Milton

Camping in Winter

The blue echo of night
faded into dawn.

I squirmed free
of my sleeping bag

like a cicada
from its crumpled skin,

emerged from the tent
into the sharp edge of winter,

trembled my way to the fire,
stepped into it,

stood among the sparks,
then burst

into wild comfortable flames
and rose

from the morning
above the grey forest.

David Evans, Jr.

Memorial Day

Well,
this is all that bloomed
of your last tree,
I know it is impossible
to soften granite
with an apple bough,
but I couldn't come
empty-handed . . .
so I'll just lay it here now
in the warm rain
and let the bees
take the last bit of pain
from the blossoms.

Carlee Swann

In the Corners of Fields

Something is calling to me
from the corners of fields,
where the leftover fence wire
suns its loose coils, and stones
thrown out of the furrow
sleep in warm litters;
where the gray faces
of old No Hunting signs
mutter into the wind,
and dry horse tanks
spout fountains of sunflowers;
where a moth
flutters in from the pasture
harried by sparrows,
and alights on a post,
so sure of its life
that it peacefully opens its wings.

Ted Kooser

The First Thanksgiving

Until the first houses could be built at
Plymouth Colony, the captain of the Mayflower
stayed in the harbor and allowed the Pilgrims
to live on board the ship.

For a long time
all we knew was the hiss
and heave of the sea
the empty shore.

Our little ship
has such a springtime name—
MAYFLOWER—like an armful
of bright blooms
from the garden!

But rocking there last fall
in the cold harbor
we wondered if a single
flower
ever grew in this hard land.

We sat chained
to the long dark days
until a warm wind
twisted sunlight through our hair
beat down on the new
rooftops.
It filled the woods with
mayflowers
and pulled green leaves
of corn
up from the earth.

Now summer has come
and gone, and we have
survived.
We give thanks.
The wind and the sea
are cold again

but fire blazes on the hearth
and the harvest is golden
in our hands.

Barbara Esbensen

Now I Know Grouse

know the legs muscled flat
against fleshless backs;
know heavy flight.
I pull feathers, snap ribs.
Blood from the thick dark breasts
stains my fingers;
a shot clinks in the sink.

I know too why you hunt them;
walking tense beside you through the trees,
all of us in line, scanning the gray grass,
ears strained for the clucking rush,
the shotgun butt, the blast.
the tumble of feathers.
Grouse hide well in the grass,
bundles of meat and feathers,
quivering with fear.

I know your squint at the sun,
how you carry a shotgun
like a pistol in one hand,
know your broad shoulders
between the rows of corn,
know how you fire without aiming,
eyes on the gray thing you love and kill;
know your brown eyes, crinkled from looking
at the sun, horizons, bottomland;
know the blue firelights in your black beard,
its crispness to my fingers.

I know how you love and kill.

Linda Hasselstrom

The Rock

There is always the rock:
That, first and last, to remember.
The rock, at times at dusk the rabbit,
Robbing the garden in its own leaden way.
And I remember how once
I lost time deliberately,
Reining the team to a stop
And raising the rock high to crush it.
Underhoof it had wanted to trip
Even the full-rumped mares,
And I stood there in the furrow
With the rock raised above my head,
Powerless at last to reduce it
Or even to lose it to sight.
Yet I tried. (For in those days
I had not learned to say
There is always the rock)
I threw it into the soft plowed ground
And dreamed that it disappeared.
How many times then it rose with the rain
I cannot say, nor can I boast
That ever its usefulness
Was fully cause for its being:
The fences failed to deplete it,
And it collared the hogs but partially.
Yet somehow I expected yesterday's blunted share
To be the last. That part which I cannot see,
I said, cannot reduce me.

William Kloefkorn

The Cottonwood,

tall twisted father,
guards the square
of the yard,
holds the light
on the undersides
of its leaves
like silver murmurs.

Its center,
split wide
by a sudden fork
of lightning,
is burned and bare.

Ask any father
why it stands there,
bent and shaking,
limbs lopped and askew—

Ask any father.

Shirley Buettner

Plains Winter

A blue ice of wind.
Snow driven forward,
sudden and shocking.
The moon is a pool
of frozen cow's milk,
set up on its edge
to shine in black sky.
These things are certain.
All else, a question.

Kenneth Mason

Approaching Winter

I

September Clouds. The first day for wearing jackets.
The corn is wandering in dark corridors,
Near the well and the whisper of tombs.

II

I sit alone surrounded by dry corn,
near the second growth of the pigweeds,
And hear the corn leaves scrape their feet on the wind.

III

Fallen ears are lying on the dusty earth.
The useful ears will lie dry in cribs, but the others, missed
By the picker, will lie here touching the ground the whole
    winter.

IV

Snow will come, and cover the husks of the fallen ears
With flakes infinitely delicate, like jewels of a murdered
    Gothic prince
Which were lost centuries ago during a great battle.

Robert Bly

Echo

Away from some empty
grade school and high school buildings

in Tulare, I stood
on the football field with my older

brother, with hands cupped around our mouths,
punishing the town's echo; I'd have believed

there was a man behind the echo
with wide eyes and a mouth in an "O"-shape,

but there were only   certain words
that passed on into the eastern sky.

I had a lot to learn about sound
and the importance

of what I sent into infinity.
We exercised

the echo, until our heads emptied
of every word that we could repeat

up there

up there   up there

Doug Cockrell

Driving Home

Driving home,
my hands correcting
the slight lateral movements
of the car on ice,
I forgot the storm
and came alive with the geese.
From a distance folded in
trees and dull hills
a sentence of wings
came toward me.
It was late afternoon.
The wind was bucking everything down,
yet I marveled at the geese
holding their V.
The point gander was true
to his long neck's motive,
the other geese were caught up
in that instinctual axis,
that old red center
which unfailingly centers
each goose, its substance
of bone and down.
And right before me,
sweeping low over the road,
those hulks of quills
climbed the telephone lines.
But they said nothing.
The wind kept riving
the cracks in the car,
the latest tunes kept rising
and falling on the latest charts,
until I awoke
and considered the distance
my hands had borne me
by themselves.

Don Welch

Land

My land, you say. You think of yellow leaves,
yellow soil under the leaves, a river yellow with silt,
summer and catfish lines and a yellow-haired girl
laughing by the river. But the year is dry,
the crops dying, corn turning yellow in the fields,
cattle listless in the bare pastures
under the yellow sun. Ah my bitter land,
you say, why do you love me so dryly.

My land's in peril, you say when you hear the shouting
and whispering, news of foreigners, news of new ideas,
when dust unfurls, raised high by marching men,
and the air above the plaza crackles with announcements.
My gentle land will be violated unless I save her.
You imagine grassy hillsides, the green sky after sunset,
a dark green rye-field with deer grazing,
tart apples and a green-eyed girl singing among the trees.

Surely my land needs me desperately at last,
you tell yourself, and someone hands you a uniform
and you go with the green men under the yellow dust
banner of drouth and loneliness, to where the air is singing
with the voice of locusts. And you lie down
beneath the dust and the grass, alone, and the river goes on
     running,
the girl laughing, the deer grazing, the land dreaming
black black black black, all the time.

Bob Ross

Windbreak

My older brother built the windbreak, in the summer of 1968, as a farm-improvement project for Future Farmers of America. It was a seven-foot-tall wall of boards, extending from one corner of the barn down along the edge of the grove for about 40 yards. The grove, aging, had lost its power against the prairie winds. The tall, thick trunks of the cottonwoods were, at last, as inefficient as telephone poles, and the cattle, in the winter, huddled cold on piles of corncobs and straw.

Cold cattle eat more. Cattle that eat more, cost more. And anyway, stopping wind on the prairie is always a noble enterprise—with literature, even, devoted to it, and with groves designed scientifically: in layers, in rows, rising from bush to shrub to small tree to large.

Growing a new grove is a years-long affair, more talked about than done. A wall of boards, which takes only a season to build, does the job less aesthetically but just as well.

No: better. My brother used tongue-in-groove boards, which sealed out that wind as effectively as glass. He made a perfect windbreak.

Which was the whole problem. If he had left gaps between the boards—if he had been willing to slow the wind down, rather than break it—my brother could have saved us all a lot of hard work. But in the heat of summer, he had forgotten, and his F.F.A. advisor had failed to remind him, that wind in the winter carries a burden of snow. And when the wind stops, it drops that burden— right on top of whatever has stopped it.

There was nothing between that windbreak and the Black Hills, nothing for 500 miles: all of South Dakota and half of Minnesota, the wind picking up snow from the draws and gullies of western South Dakota, from the Missouri River valley, from the level plains of eastern South Dakota, rangeland and farmland, grass and hay and cornstalks and flat, black plowland—howling into Minnesota with its load, whistling and hooting, freight-laden and full.

Then it hit that windbreak.

And dropped that snow like lead.

Five hundred miles of snow piled up around that windbreak. My brother received the farm-improvement award that year—but really, he should have left gaps between the boards. He should have let part of the wind through, so that the drift would form 10 feet east of the windbreak. Without those gaps, the snow covered the windbreak and got so crusted-over and hard that the cattle could walk right over it, right out of the feedlot and into the grove. And from there, if they wanted, they could go anywhere.

So we spent a lot of time shoveling snow away from that windbreak, the sting of ice in our faces. Many times every winter, grumbling and complaining, we dug deep snow-trenches into the drift on the leeward side of the windbreak. After a night of wind, when our regular chores were done, the cattle fed and content, our father would gather us together and find a shovel for each of us, and we would trudge to the windbreak and dig.

And every time we did, our father would at some point pause and lean on his shovel, and we would all take that as a signal to do likewise, and we'd gaze at the cattle, and then Dad would observe that there really should be gaps between the boards of that windbreak. Nothing more; just an observation. Then he'd return to work, and we'd reluctantly do the same, until we had finally dug a six-foot-deep trench extending the length of the barrier. If we were lucky, there wouldn't be another big wind for several days, and the trench would last long enough to make our work seem worthwhile, the cattle climbing up the crusted snow to stare dumbly out of white faces at this angular gap where flowing snow should be.

But the trench always filled in again—sometimes overnight, sometimes a month later. It always filled in again, and we always dug it out again, repeating what was, to us, a wearisome and useless task. Strangely, we never blamed our brother for the extra work. We appreciated the windbreak for its kindness to the cattle. But we grew frustrated at the futility of challenging wind. We came to see the wind as insistent on undoing our labors.

In our father's voice, we never heard anger or frustration as he leaned on his shovel and gazed at the cattle. His voice was always mild, merely making an observation: Gaps between the boards would save us all this work. But it wasn't as if he minded the work; it wasn't as if it bothered him.

I understand some things now, I think, that I didn't understand then. My father knew that on the prairie, only the wind is permanent. We were trying to frustrate the wind; the wind wasn't trying to frustrate us. The difference between those two viewpoints is a great one, and I think now that maybe he was trying to teach us that difference.

In his early twenties, he had taken over the family farm from his father, who had made poor decisions and accumulated bad debts. My father worked long hours to keep the farm from bankruptcy. It hadn't been his intention to farm. He had thought to take up a career in business—had gone to two years of business school, even. But he did what he had to do, paid off those debts, maintained the farm. And he was a good farmer: careful, deliberate, in love with the land. If he had regrets about returning to the farm, he never let them show to his children.

His father died, and then his mother, and through complications of estate settlement which I've never quite understood, the land was divided between him and his six brothers and sisters. None of the others wanted to farm, so my father had to buy their shares from them. In truth, he bought that land twice: once to rescue it from his own father's bad debts, and once to claim it as his own.

The second buying had a great influence on him—not in the form of bitterness, but in the form of caution. He bought no land after that—though he had some opportunities, though it would have made good sense. He stayed with the 200 acres that contained so much of his sweat, and he managed to raise nine children on that land and keep them, for the most part, oblivious to their near-poverty.

He managed, finally, to own the farm outright. Then, only a few years later, before he could even enjoy the respite, he died, brought down by a stroke, this careful and deliberate and intelligent man who planted corn rows so straight that they diminished like railroad tracks clear down to the far fenceline. For a year his sons went on farming the land, often staying home from school to get the work done. And we farmed it, actually, quite successfully and well. We had had good training.

But that larger wind, of which the snow-laden wind of the prairie is sign and symbol, that wind of time and mortality and fate, propels us all differently, and we sensed, with regret, that we could not continue our father's livelihood. We could not, or would not, save the farm from his death as he had saved it from his own father's debts. We had an auction, sold the machinery, rented the land out. Eventually my mother moved into town, partly for protection from the winter winds that might so easily leave her stranded in a snowbank over a lonely road. And then, finally, after family discussion, long-distance phone calls—we were, by now, making our livings all over the country— we sold the land to some neighbors.

That is land for which my father paid twice. In the end, he failed to keep it for his children. But I think of him leaning on his shovel in the trench of that windbreak, and I know: not failed. To view it as failure is to take the view of my childhood: that the wind is frustrating us. He knew, as we didn't, that we were frustrating wind. He must also have known, I imagine, that though he finally owned the land, it never belonged to him, just as it does not belong to those who own it now.

His children, forming our own lives over half the United States, belong to the land and the wind. We carry part of our father with us as we are swept along. We no longer shovel out windbreaks. But the memory remains, and we hold onto it, tight, in the wind.

No one shovels out my brother's windbreak, though it must be stopping snow as well as ever. For now, on that farm, there are no cattle to contain, and the snow curves gracefully over the windbreak, shapeless like natural things, without neat, straight trenches carved into it. Finally, that's all right.

It's a fine thing, after all, to shovel snow blown from half a continent, while white-faced cattle gaze over your shoulder. And it's good to realize, and accept, that the 500-mile wind will always return, that the trench—no matter how deep, how straight, how square—will be filled in again, will return to its original formlessness.

For a long time, I could not understand my father's acceptance of a problem so easily solved: his simple refusal to knock every second board out of the windbreak. I didn't understand how he could state and restate a solution to our problem, and an easy solution at that—and yet, year after year, refuse to implement it. Even that is beginning to make sense to me now.

The nuns taught us that perfection is impossible in this world, though it must continually be striven for. My father's attitude toward the windbreak teaches a different lesson, and perhaps a truer one: Perfection is possible in this world, though it can be maintained in small things only, and even that is struggle, with repercussions one cannot expect—but once you achieve perfection in small things, you don't back away from it simply because you discover the magnitude of the work required to maintain it.

My brother built a perfect windbreak!

He defied the nuns, and built it.

And my father then enlisted hours and hours and hours of our help to struggle against the repercussions of that perfection.

Because once you achieve it, that perfection, you maintain it. You don't knock boards out just to save yourself some work.

I haven't entirely learned these lessons. I can state them, but I still grumble a lot in the trench. I have doubts and uncertainties about what I say next here. But I know that my father didn't, and wouldn't. And maybe that is enough:

As the 500-mile wind has scattered his children into our individual draws and gullies, so it will gather us together. As it whirls the world in seeming chaos, so it will straighten all out. There is a barrier somewhere at the end of it, a barrier that breaks it, but one designed by a wiser architect than my brother. And when, like snow, we drop gently out of the wind, we will find Dad there, no longer needing a shovel amid perfect formless things, mild, and awaiting his family.

Kent Meyers

Letting The Wind Talk

Some time ago a small creek I live near was turned into a ditch, the trees pushed over and the bottom dredged deeper so the water wouldn't loiter on its way to the Gulf of Mexico. For years it had remained, a ragged piece of leftover prairie coming in and out of the morning mist very much like a ghost, reminding people of a different time, until it got on everyone's nerves and the bulldozers were called in to civilize it.

It was a modest stream, long incorporated into the county drainage system, but to me, at the time, it was the wilderness. On one of its banks was a tiny stretch of virgin prairie, blooming with flowers and bluestem. When the heavy equipment moved out in the fall, there was a gouge in the earth where the creek had been and the trees were piled to one side, the dry leaves still chattering in the autumn wind. The grassy banks had become frozen mud. There was nothing left for the mink. The creek was officially a ditch. Ice had formed over the shallow water. It didn't take much arithmetic to multiply the new ditch by a million times and know what had happened to the prairie.

The prairie is changing again. A hundred years after it was originally broken it is being broken once more. The small farm is going under the plow to join the prairie grass. And the prairie children, now white, are scattered like the Indian, the buffalo and the horse-high bluestem.

I stood in the doorway of the farm house. It was abandoned, the windows punched out. For a while it had been used by migrant workers who weeded the nearby sugar beet fields, but it was alone now, sitting on the gravelly ridge that was the old beach of ancient Lake Agassiz. Looking out over the flat lake bottom, I tried to imagine water and waves lapping the gravel, but there was only the endless, freshly plowed wheat field that each year moved closer to the gravel ridge. Soon it would throw its black waves over the old farm house.

Inside, the floors were covered with beat-up mattresses and the walls filled with religious pictures and Catholic church schedules. In the kitchen cupboard were three or four half-full bottles of chili sauce. On the porch there were at least ten hoes left behind, the handles almost black with use. Nailed to the outside of the house was a sign warning an imaginary visitor to beware of a phantom dog.

The autumn grass was full of tall weeds that had climbed up onto the beach from the old lake. Ragweed and Russian Thistle surrounded the house and the other rundown, silent buildings. From the edge of the house I could see rain clouds coming from the west, they dropped low, almost touching the dry lake bed. The wind carried the dark smell of water ahead of the blackening clouds as rain began to fall a mile away. I saw the old lake wet again and shining in the dreary gray afternoon as the lake bottom woke up and stirred, almost remembering what it had been. The gravel moved under my feet.

The farm boy who once lived there is by now a man, probably working in a factory in a distant city or maybe he has been allowed a visit to the middle-class and owns a camper or he might not have any ambitions at all and goes from job to job, unable to get the sound of the prairie wind out of his head. When the rain reached me, the cold drops went through my jacket.

Although outwardly transformed and broken, as a horse is broken, and saddled with farms and mortgages, nothing can fill the empty space of the prairie sky and horizon. Not the acres of crops that have replaced the long grass, not the few lonesome hand-planted trees or the farms with shiny silos, not even the dusty towns that want to be cities and do their best by putting up junk food restaurants and turning on lots of lights in the dark prairie night.

Space is the great characteristic of the prairie. In it every individual, every tree, each rock and piece of grass has its own sky. The grass and rocks accept the emptiness, even thrive, but the people want to be in groups and are seldom seen standing by themselves. In the days of the settlers, many went mad and were unable to get the sound of the western Minnesota wind out of their heads until they died. But some of them found they had strange feelings for the uniqueness of the place, a fascination for the prairie similar to that the mountain men had for the wilds of the Rocky Mountains. In China the British called it going native, the thing most dreaded by colonial people. On the prairie the symptoms were the ability to be alone, the urge to go on long walks in the tall friendly grass, and the desire to forget the values of civilization.

Now, a century later, most of us born here don't know prairie grass when we see it. But sometimes the old feeling is there, in the prairie wind and the call of the migrating goose over the melting snow. Then you will see a farmer walking alone over his muddy fields pretending that he is deciding what to plant. Inside, no one can concentrate. The blue sky comes in both windows. The damp smell of prairie spring comes up to the back door and feet start to itch. It no longer seems such a threat to be just a speck on the prairie horizon. It is possible then, to stand like the pine tree, another foreigner on the

continued . . .

prairie, without moving much through blizzard, rain or sunshine, satisfied to be in one spot, letting the wind do all the talking.

Along an isolated fence row the prairie is alive in the quiet wild rose. It's as though the soul of the prairie went underground when the sod was turned. Now it surfaces here and there in an unpretentious flower or a small slough of incredibly blue water, lifting the teal gently through a long afternoon. These are small things, gifts the prairie still gives willingly to those who stop greasing their machinery long enough on a spring morning to look up at the geese flying high.

Geese and spring take the prairie closest to its origins; for a while it is like its old self. It is the time when the air has been scrubbed clean by new rain and you can see all the way to Manitoba. The immense sky becomes even larger to make room for all the spring sunlight, the ponds are the deepest blue that they will ever be the whole year, and the earth, shy about showing the first green shoots of grass, needs to be coaxed along by the warm west wind. And the land fills with thousands of ephemeral potholes like patches of blue sky that have dropped to earth.

Tom Hennen

Additional Readings

From *The Golden Bowl*

Twisting its way down through fat bluffs, the AYP Highway reaches the Big Sioux River, crosses it, and enters western Siouxland. It runs straight west across prairie farmland toward a cloud of treetops on the far horizon, which, lengthening, become towering cottonwoods. In the cool shade of the trees the pastures are green.

The Atlantic-Yellowstone-Pacific Highway slows for a country filling station, bumps across a railroad track, and veers northwest. It makes a beeline straight for a mirage of icicles, which, lifting, become the steeples and smokestacks of Sioux Falls. In the early morning light the downtown towers are pink.

The Highway enters the city, glides down a long hill past humble worker cottages, swoops briefly over a viaduct, slips between gaudy supermarkets housed behind the false fronts of old stores, pauses beside the pink stone walls of a venerable library, runs beneath high arching elms, passes through a district of tall white frame dwellings with green lawns, and then, abruptly leaving the city behind, sprints westward across slowly sliding prairie land.

The country continues to show green. Only here and there a yellow blade of grass or a shriveled leaf of corn flecks through. For a few miles, too, the farm buildings glow with good paint and shining window panes. And the cylinders of water towers, looming above the little towns in the distance, are as glossy black as new stovepipe hats.

But farther on, the land loses its healthy green. Much of the grass is pale and many of the cornstalks are yellow and dead. Some are even burnt brown. The water towers and windmills, and the barns and silos and houses and coops, and privies within the windbreaks, are more drab, more deserted, the paint more chipped and gray.

Still farther on, gray dust films everything, even the moving things. When the wind comes the old structures shrug a little and the gray silt slides off in shivers. And sometimes, when a rain comes, the old buildings stand forlorn amidst the rustling of strange greens.

The Highway lopes through this land, curving sometimes, and cutting sharply, but always running west. It passes dying Siouxland farms and bonesharp people. It spans the dry beds of vanished rivers marked only by rows of leafless trees. It crosses the lazy Jim River, asleep in the roomy bed once occupied by the old Missouri. It circles empty lakebeds lying cracked and ugly, and only a little damp, like the crusting sores of eczema. It passes dry wallows where, centuries ago

continued . . .

when the land was covered with knife-edged prairie grass, buffalo bulls bellowed and gored each other.

Still farther on, where Siouxland leaves off and the real Dakotas begin, empty wells pit the land. Rotting bodies of dead animals lie facing empty water tanks. Skeletons of farms lie quietly in dusty slumber. Machines, the levers once warm with the cupped hands of men, stand idle, rusting, blackening.

Fissures in the land as deep and wide as glacier crevasses open the soil to the wind. Cracks wide enough to swallow cows zigzag across the earth like strokes of black lightning. The earth, like a colossal apple hurled upon the floor of the universe, has burst open, its fragments scattering to the winds.

Suddenly the Highway comes to where the Missouri River has gouged a deep diagonal wrinkle across the belly of the Dakotas. It dips sharply into a small valley, pushes through a little town, and hastens to the edge of the Missouri River banks. A bridge arches over the racing tan waters and on the other side the road climbs again and moves steadily westward.

It rolls through a land heaving with an ocean's undulation. It skirts the edge of Big Foot Hill, where a spur drops abruptly into the yawning, rasp-rough mouth of the Bad Lands to snake its way among myriads of red-yellow teeth.

At last, near the western border of the Dakotas, the Highway moves quietly beneath the blue pines of the Black Hills.

Frederick Manfred

Four Poems by Ted Kooser

The Salesman

Today he's wearing his vinyl shoes,
shiny and white as little Karmann Ghias
fresh from the body shop, and as he moves
in his door-to-door glide, these shoes fly round
each other, honking the horns of their soles.
His hose are black and ribbed and tight, as thin
as an old umbrella or the wing of a bat.
(They leave a pucker when he pulls them off.)
He's got on his double-knit leisure suit
in a pond-scum green, with a tight white belt
that matches his shoes but suffers with cracks
at the golden buckle. His shirt is brown
and green, like a pile of leaves, and it opens
onto the neck at a Brillo pad
of graying hair which tosses a cross and chain
as he walks. The collar is splayed out over
the jacket's lapels yet leaves a lodge pin
taking the sun like a silver spike.
He's swinging a briefcase full of the things
of this world, a leather cornucopia
heavy with promise. Through those dark lenses,
each of the doors along your sunny street
looks slightly ajar, and in your quiet house
the dog of your willpower cowers and growls,
then crawls in under the basement steps,
making the jingle of coin with its tags.

Living Near the Rehabilitation Home

Tonight she is making her way
up the block by herself, throwing
her heavy shoes from step to step,
her lunchbox swinging out wide
with a rhythmical clunk, each bone
on its end and feebly bending
into her pitiful gait. Where is
her friend tonight, the idiot boy?
Each day at this time I see them
walking together, his bright red jacket
trying the dusk, her old blue coat
his shadow. She moves too slowly
for him, and he breaks from her hand
and circles her in serious orbits,
stamping his feet in the grass.
Perhaps they have taken him elsewhere
to live. From high on my good legs
I imagine her lonely without him,
but perhaps she's happy at last.

Houses at the Edge of Town

These are the houses of farmers
retired from their fields;
white houses, freshly folded
and springing open again
like legal papers. These are houses
drawn up on the shore of the fields,
their nets still wet,
the fishermen sleeping curled in the bows.
See how the gardens
wade into the edge of the hayfield,
the cucumbers crawling out under the lilacs
to lie in the sun.

The Red Wing Church

There's a tractor in the doorway of a church
in Red Wing, Nebraska, in a coat of mud
and straw that drags the floor. A broken plow
sprawls beggarlike behind it on some planks
that make a sort of roadway up the steps.
The steeple's gone. A black tar-paper scar
that lightning might have made replaces it.
They've taken it down to change the house of God
to Homer Johnson's barn, but it's still a church,
with clumps of tiger lilies in the grass
and one of those boxlike, glassed-in signs
that give the sermon's topic (reading now
a bird's nest and a little broken glass).
The good works of the Lord are all around:
the steeple top is standing in a garden
just up the alley; it's a hen house now:
fat leghorns gossip at its crowded door.
Pews stretch on porches up and down the street,
the stained-glass windows style the mayor's house,
and the bell's atop the firehouse in the square.
The cross is only God knows where.

Ted Kooser

Three Poems by Robert Bly

A Man Writes to a Part of Himself

What cave are you in, hiding, rained on?
Like a wife, starving, without care,
Water dripping from your head, bent
Over ground corn . . .

      You raise your face into the rain
That drives over the valley—
Forgive me, your husband,
On the streets of a distant city, laughing,
With many appointments,
Though at night going also
To a bare room, a room of poverty,
To sleep among a bare pitcher and basin
In a room with no heat—

      Which of us two then is the worse off?
And how did this separation come about?

Sunset at a Lake

      The sun is sinking. Here, on the pine-haunted bank, the mosquitoes fly around drowsily, and moss stands out as if it wanted to speak. Calm falls on the lake, which now seems heavier and inhospitable. Far out, rafts of ducks drift like closed eyes, and a thin line of silver caused by something invisible slowly moves toward shore in the viscous darkness under the southern bank. Only a few birds, the troubled ones, speak to the darkening roof of earth; small weeds stand abandoned, the clay is sending her gifts back to the center of the earth.

Driving Toward the Lac Qui Parle River

I

I am driving; it is dusk; Minnesota.
The stubble field catches the last growth of sun.
The soybeans are breathing on all sides.
Old men are sitting before their houses on carseats
In the small towns. I am happy,
the moon rising above the turkey sheds.

II

The small world of the car
Plunges through the deep fields of the night,
On the road from Willmar to Milan.
This solitude covered with iron
Moves through the fields of night
Penetrated by the noise of crickets.

III

Nearly to Milan, suddenly a small bridge,
And water kneeling in the moonlight.
In small towns the houses are built right on the ground;
the lamplight falls on all fours in the grass.
When I reach the river, the full moon covers it;
a few people are talking low in a boat.

Robert Bly

Two Poems by Bill Holm

Though difficult, it is possible to kill boxelder bugs.
If you are interested, you might try this method

Take two bricks.
Creep deliberately up
Behind the boxelder bug,
Being careful not to sing—
This will alert him.
In a graceful flowing gesture,
Something like a golf swing
Or reaching for your lover in the dark,
Gather up the boxelder bug
On the surface of the left brick
Bringing the right brick
At the same time firmly down
Together with the left brick.
There will be a loud crashing,
Like broken cymbals,
Maybe a breaking of brick, and
If you are not careful,
Your own voice rising.
When the brick dust has settled
And you have examined your own hands,
Carefully,
You will not see the boxelder bug.
There is a small hole in the brick
And he is exploring it,
Calmly, like a millionaire
In an antique shop.

Nuclear physicists use astounding comparisons
to make clear the nature of infinite numbers

An adult male Norwegian
weighs as much as
two and a half billion
boxelder bugs.
Is it any surprise that
there are more boxelder bugs
than Norwegians?
Imagine a planet in which
Norwegians crawled up
and down your kitchen walls
by the thousands, hid
under the warm coffee pot,
fell like discolored noodles out
of the noodle bags where they slept;
after the blizzards started,
you would find Norwegians
dried inside light fixtures, Norwegians
clogging up the vacuum cleaner,
Norwegians floating in
cups of lukewarm coffee.

Bill Holm

Monsieur

My French teacher Minnie Miller
says I have the wrong facial makeup
to pronounce *monsieur.*
She is tall, thin, ancient,
her lips a perpetual pucker,
her fingers
like those bones of that skeleton
they scared you half to death with
in grade school.

These are the fingers
she presses against my face,
rearranging the cockeyed structure
of my southcentral Kansas pronunciation.
Monsieur. Say it again, Mr. Hayseed,
this time more deliberately. *Monsieur.*
I say it again and again,
each time more slowly
than the time before,
the fingers of Minnie Miller
adjusting my jaw, my cheekbones,
my hayseed lips
until I swear
I'll not be fit for anything
tonight, least of all
that girl with the dark moony eyes
who when at last I asked her out
said yes. *Oui. Oui, monsieur,*
until the hand relents and

mon Dieu! my own face returns and
evening happens,
dark moony eyes
above the menu at Harold's Place,
around us in the soft blue light
the aromatic babble of perfect strangers.

William Kloefkorn

Three Poems by David Allan Evans

Rakers

It's the Saturday my wife gets that look:
responsible as storm windows, as cleaned-out
garages: things to be hung up on nails on the
walls, cement floors swept clean so cars can
roll in shiningly over them. That October
look. Then my daughter mentions all the leaves
in the front yard, all the neighbors out raking;
asks where the dumb rake is.

But I won't be raking today.

I won't be having the garbage man in the
morning pitching the black plastic lawn bags
with twist tops in the hydraulic truck and
thinking, *He's a raker too.*

Raking's one more deadly habit I can do
without. I know it can get too natural, automatic
and genetic. One day my grandson picks up his
little play rake, his friends catch on, and
soon everybody is doing it. Then a kid down
the block is born with a rake for a hand. That's
neighborhood evolution carried too far. Everybody at the first of October standing around
leaning on rakes and staring up at the trees
with open mouths, waiting for leaf rain.

I Can See Why

Once (I read this in the paper)
a man in a utility shack
up in northern North Dakota
in a blizzard,
looked out his window and
saw a 500-foot television
tower collapse and fall.

He said he heard nothing,
only watched how
"the thing fell in slow motion."

Knowing about Dakota blizzards
I can see why.
You might as well be listening
from your grave—
you might as well be
a deaf man in a lifeboat
watching the Titanic go under.

I envy the man in the shack,
and the imagined man
in the lifeboat.

The sound of snapping cables,
of steel crashing on steel,
yells for help—all this is
plainly redundant.

There are some things
only the eyes should feed on.

April's Carnival

Once, a boy in Sioux City,
after rain washed out a carnival,
I stopped by the Ferris Wheel turning
with empty chairs and no
lights for coloring a nickel
sky, turning with nobody
under it working the levers—

Then I saw him: bare-chested,
a young worker preferring to
ride as he dismantled his ride,
standing up inside the steel
spokes with a monkey wrench,
a cigarette stuck on his bottom
lip, loosening the bolts on
the chairs, climbing against
the clockwise wheeling or relaxing
and going with it, taking a long
drag as he fell in a curve and
curving under and up and
over the trees and down—

That quiet turning, that wheel was
his alone, to *leave be* or
dismantle, hanging on with one
hand, riding as he worked and
working as he rode, bare-chested,
standing up on the Ferris Wheel turning
with empty chairs and no
lights for coloring a nickel
sky, after the rain washed out
April's carnival, still turning.

David Allan Evans

Carnivore

The fat bus swings to the curb
and excretes people.
No one waits
to be fed to it.
Disgusted, it grunts
and lurches off to hunt again.

John Calvin Rezmerski

The Big Snapper

Abner McCann was a well-known poacher. O, he'd been pinched a couple times. Where it hurt. For a poor man that's the pocket book.

Abner was a bustling, compact man with bright blue eyes. That sometimes rolled white and a little crazy. In his younger days, he was famous around here as an all-around athlete. In his late forties, he kept some renown alive by maintaining a running battle with the game warden.

One afternoon in mid May, after school, I rowed a small duck boat up the wide inlet which enters the south side of Richardson. Schools of bass were gliding through the spring run-off water beneath me. That water was so clear it felt strange to be on it. As if I was floating on air.

I quit rowing. Sat in the bottom of the boat, legs stretched out, leaning against the back seat. Listened to a slough pumper, listened to a meadowlark, listened to breeding frogs and blackbirds and the rustling of the reeds. Got lost somewhere wonderful. Then the rustling of the reeds got louder. Something big was crashing through them. I'd been warned about a Holstein bull that pastured there. I rose quickly from the bottom of the boat. Got ready to row.

It wasn't a bull, but Abner McCann. Wearing hip boots. He was thrashing through the cattails, out to the edge of the open water. He all but ignored me. Climbed onto a muskrat house. Stood there, staring into the water, a fish spear in one hand and a dip net in the other. Then he spoke, and his voice was urgent and conspiratorial. As if he was maybe trying to get a young woman to share a bottle of whiskey with him. But there was also the tone of command in his voice:

"Joe, you get on over here. Row me along the edge of these rushes, an' I'll stab us some bass."

I hesitated a second. The bass season wasn't yet open, and it was illegal to spear them anyway. Then I pushed over to Abner and he clambered aboard. The first thing we saw was an enormous snapping turtle. Wavering along through the clear water just above the bottom. Little clouds of swamp muck rising in its wake.

"Put your back into it," hissed Abner.

Turtles *were* legal. I pulled hard and caught up to it. Abner's movements were quick and jerky. And very sure. In the space of a sparrow's chirp, he'd slipped his net over that turtle and jerked it tight. With a grunt, he lifted it. Water draining from net and turtle. He inverted the net and shook. And the snapper, maybe a thirty-pounder, fell through. Its claws caught for a second in the net. Then, thud! it hit the bottom of the boat. Legs and tail and neck thrashing around like a bunch of heavy-bodied snakes. Hissing. The long neck lashed out maybe fifteen inches. Its beak snapped the air. Me sitting there barefoot.

"*Criminy, Abner!*"

I jumped to the back of the boat. Shoved the snapper away from me with an oar. it struck at the heel of Abner's hipboot. But didn't get a grip. Abner, spear up, had his eye on three bass out in front of us, hanging alongside a sunken log.

"Just pull ahead, real easy. But not right at—"

I was trying to turn the snapper onto its back. When Abner stopped talking. Then I heard it, too. The roar of a big outboard motor. A power boat was coming straight at us. Full-throttle from the north side of the lake. Its nose was high in the air. Coming at us, it bounced and splashed like a heavy-boned loon trying to rise from the water.

"*The game warden!*" hissed Abner.

Violently, he threw his spear, then his net. As far as he could into the cattails. Shoving the turtle away from me with an oar, I leaned far out over the gunwale to keep the boat from tipping. Which wasn't to Abner's advantage. Off balance, from heaving his net, he hung for a second on one foot, waving frantically, angrily at me with his right hand. But, with the turtle between us, there was no hope of helping him. He teetered farther. Then the boat slipped out from under him and he hit the water with a loud flop. There was a lot of churning around down there under the water. Then Abner broke back through the surface with a gargling roar. Clouds of mud rose around him in the water. His eyes rolled wild.

"Sorry, Abner!"

I thought he was going to tip the boat on me. For spite. But the power boat was still roaring down on us from the north. And Abner was just doing his damnedest to get out of there. He made it to the cattails. Thrashed through them. As if driven by an engine himself. His blue stocking cap gone, I could see the bald spot toward the back of his head. Rising up and down in the cattails. Then he was charging across the pasture, up into the woods.

I was left there to face whatever the oncoming music. And to wrestle that enormous and angry turtle. I gave up on trying to keep it. Gripped it by the tail and swung it overboard.

At the same time, almost to the entrance of the inlet, the power boat swung east and around. Began bucketing back north again. Just as I'd thought. It wasn't the game warden at all. It was a red and white boat. A game warden's would be green or brown.

I watched the turtle peddling away through the mud-clouded

water. For a second I wished I'd kept it. Then I just let the idea go. Leaned back and wondered about my three-minute interlude with Abner McCann.

"Jeez! What a guy!"

Actually, I felt great about it all. Was looking forward to telling Dad. But the sun was lulling me. The power boat had stopped and things had gone so silent. Except for the sweet little sounds emerging around me again. The humming, whistling and groaning of a warm spring afternoon. I lay back on the bottom of the boat. Sent myself up into the sky. Schools of bass sailing beneath me. Closed my eyes to the too-complicated dream in which I was living. Floated free in the real for a while.

Joe Paddock

Drawing Swastikas on the Fogged Windows of St. Joseph's Grade School, 1959

After school we cleaned bruised boards,
clapped white explosions from erasers.
The nun sat in her solitude;
in ours, we drew bombers in notebooks.

Sisters, we meant nothing by it.
We were apprentices at war—
grey blood something that grinned at us from the screen.
Buds on the girls and triggers excited us.
We dreamed Nazis: how they could scrape off
the horizon with their fingernails.

We didn't understand the world
was once a mountain, ready to avalanche.
For us history was that pine forest
behind the playground, filling with snow.

Noon hours in the basement,
we rationed cigarettes, laughed
at bomb shelter signs, fingered dirty pictures

continued . . .

smuggled in bag lunches
until the boilers hissed.

After an hour she dismissed us.
We saw fish in the aquarium by the cloakroom
swimming in squadrons.
At home we drew on our arms with red Magic Marker.

Sisters, no enemy planes ever tore the air
above your school. It was just a target
for the wrecking ball, a decade later.
When the first bricks collapsed,
ghosts of the kids we once were
    cowered in the basement,
        the lights blacked out,
            the windows steamed.

Bill Meissner

Night Lyric

Eerie, eerie, the wind in the limbs says.
Hoot-owls mock the mice. The worn-out snow
grunts like tired horses.
I haunt the grove in awkward, tearing cold.

Weed-stalks tick and buzz.
Some still have crowns. The seed I jolt
skids like dust under the trees,
a line of twisted 80-year-old willows.

Starlight and snowlight soften a stucco house.
December, 1943.
One yellow window. Midnight yowls and roars.
A woman *hoohs* the lamp out,
smoke jitters downwind from the chimney.
This frost breaks iron. I have no business here.

Bob Ross

Two Poems by Thomas McGrath

Such Lies They Told Us

In memory, the wild blue geese, lagging behind the spring,
Seemed all summer long to acclaim our extravagant
  unselfish notions
Of time—for they seemed eternal, each locked to its
  changeless image
On the lost lake of the past. And under the dead sun,
Those kissing hours of illusion blessed our foreheads
  forever—
Or so we thought. For the years, opening their windows on
That tame image of life, promised the use of our powers—
Such lies were told us. Signs seen later made us unsure.
In the first fall frost the wild geese flew up, circled, were gone.

Nobody put us wise. There came a sound of crying
But we didn't know it as ours as we lay on the cold white
  table
Till the banker came in with a knife and that terrible look
  in his eyes.
And the judge sent his wicked little men in through the ports
  of childhood
To cut off the hands of our play and steal the ticket to Pueblo.
In our youth we heard the footsteps whispering up to
  the door
And the landlord's son came in, wearing the false face of
  kindness,
Talking of brotherhood. Later, waiting in darkness,
His gunmen coughed in the alley. But nobody spoke of
  that war

Into which the poor are born with their eyes blindfolded.
Though many will spend their lives, lost on mortgaged acres,
Shiver in the winds of their weakness, or, on the home quarter
Open their eyes among murderers one day on the summer
  fallow—
You may not bandage those wounds: allow the light to enter.
Wisdom comes from the struggle, creating the courage
  and grace

continued . . .

Which under the animal sun, in a world wilder than geese,
Still lets our eyes embrace for the proud and final time
When capital's sickly sheriff drops the hood on your face.

The Roads Into the Country

Ran only in one direction, in childhood years—
Into mysterious counties, beyond the farm or the town,
Toward the parish of desire the roads led up or down
Past a thicket of charms, a river of wishing hours,

Till, wrapt in a plenum of undying sun
We heard the tick of air-guns on the hills.
The pheasant stalked by on his gilded heels,
The soft-eyed foxes from the woods looked on,

While hung upon the blue wall of the air
The hawk stared down into a sea of fire,
Where, salamanders in our element,
We ate the summer like a sacrament.

That was in memory's country, and is lost.
The roads led nowhere. Aloof in his field of fire
The hawk wheels pitiless. Alone, afar,
The skirmishers of childhood hurry past,

Hunting a future that they cannot will.
Children of light, travelling our darkened years
We cannot warn them. Distant, they have no ears
For those they will become. Across a wall

Of terror and innocence we hear the voice,
The air-gun in the land of all mock-choice;
Around us not the game of fox and pheasant,
But the gunfire of the real and terrible present.

Thomas McGrath

On Highway 212, West of Faith, South Dakota

for a child

Trusting our tired, ill-designed
knees, you raise your arms
and wait patiently
to be lifted, carried.
You trust us again,
falling asleep in the car:
knowing we'll keep you safe,
covering a distance
you know nothing of.

We've set a thread of asphalt
on this prairie;
fence made of wire,
tree limbs and railroad ties
wavering into shadow,
to tell us what we own.

That neat link fence
was built to government specifications.
Its nuclear missiles
would rise out of nightmare if they could:
telling us why we must,
telling us how we need them.

Soon you'll wake confused
in the fast-moving car.
You'll be alone,
there will be miles or more
between us:
trust the world.

Kathleen Norris

The Insurance Men

On the counter a temple of dishes
throws back the afternoon light
and we are happy like this,

but you must leave the kitchen
to join my hand when they sit down
with us.

One's sober as death.
He looks modeled out of clay or wax.
His smile seems broken through hard rock
to reach his face.
The effect is painful,
what they want.

The other, fat, gesticulates,
although he doesn't have the facts
(the other holds the book like a name book—
the cover is black)
he argues for commitment.
He says, "Suppose an early death"
and tries to lead me
while I live to see you Barb
and Jackie eating grass
or bleared by shame,
the Mustang getting towed away
to please a creditor.

"Suppose a death at fifty-five
when the policy's matured."
(I see it in my top drawer
swollen like a leech
or spilling dimes into the corners.)
I get a double figure then
to get me buried right;
my child, supposing one,
through college, or supposing two,
well on their way,
and time for Barb to get arranged.

He finishes, and no one speaks.
The light is flaking from the trees.
We huddle in the shade like sheep.
I realize why they pick the afternoons.

Frightened by the failing light
I almost think I've lost my chance.
I almost nod, but check the other
for some sign.
His smile's still there, a dog's
persistent snout. There is no
stopping it. Like death itself
it finds the air, my hands, our daughter's
upturned face, our fragile lives.

There's nothing we can do.
We let them out
and sit there in the dark.

Greg Kuzma

Appointed Rounds

At first he refused to deliver junk mail because it was stupid, all those deodorant ads, money-making ideas and contests. Then he began to doubt the importance of the other mail he carried. He began to randomly select first class mail for non-delivery. After he had finished his mail route each day he would return home with his handful of letters and put them in the attic, he didn't open them and never even looked at them again. It was as if he were an agent of Fate, capricious and blind. In the several years before he was caught, friends vanished, marriages failed, business deals fell through. Toward the end he became more and more bold, deleting houses, then whole blocks from his route. He began to feel he'd been born in the wrong era. If only he could have been a Pony Express rider galloping into some prairie town with an empty bag or the runner from Marathon collapsing in the streets of Athens, gasping, "No news."

Louis Jenkins

Great Uncle Harm

That year in December the winds
came down like lean white wolves
aching for any kind of meat.
On New Year's Eve day
they found Great Uncle Harm
on the old Ackermann place,
washed up by a flood
of homemade tomato wine
against the frozen cornstalks,
his hand gripping the bottle
like roots around a stone.
They laid him in the corn crib
to keep the body cold.
Uncle Harm was stored there
two days, waiting for the coroner,
his teeth like hybrid kernels
past dent stage, his hair
blowing like dried cornsilk
on last summer's husks.

S. C. Hahn

Clara: In the Post Office

I keep telling you, I'm not a feminist.
I grew up an only child on a ranch,
so I drove tractors, learned to ride.
When the truck wouldn't start, I went to town
for parts. The man behind the counter
told me I couldn't rebuild a carburetor.
I could: every carburetor on the place. That's
necessity, not feminism.
                        I learned to do the books
after my husband left me and the debts
and the children. I shoveled snow and pitched hay
when the hired man didn't come to work.
I learned how to pull a calf
when the vet was too busy. As I thought,
the cow did most of it herself; they've been
birthing alone for ten thousand years. Does
that make them feminists?
                        It's not
that I don't like men; I love them—when I can.
But I've stopped counting on them
to change my flats or open my doors.
That's not feminism; that's just good sense.

                        Linda Hasselstrom

Self-Portrait

Here's a man bearing great weight.
Notice how the shoulders slide and sink,
how the back rolls them forward
as the back rolls, as maybe
a support collapses and his height
avalanches an inch.
He carries a small chest,
one so narrow
you'd sooner snap it
like a twig than hold it long—
he is no stick to walk with.
Was a time his belly was flat,
but paunched now,
the weight silts to the bottom
of his stomach's lake.
His legs are serviceable, though stilts.
His arms, his hands, his feet,
his tubular neck, leftover parts.
You can see his face sag,
around those tired-green eyes,
at his lips, that drawn purse.
His beard is dirty water,
and just beneath
the white trough along the curb.
His hair, loose, runs all directions.
It can't get far enough away.

Mark Sanders

Looking for Your Blue Spot

We always heard
Oriental babies have blue spots,
blue splotches of pigment
on their brown bottoms

so at your first bath
we turned you over.
There glowed a blue quarter
at the base of your spine
like a scar
where someone snipped off your tail

and higher up
indigo Madagascar
floated alone.

These blue markings grew,
stretched out
bath by bath
until invisible
except for a certain sheen.

Now we play the game

Where is your blue spot?

You grab your pants
and run giggling through the hall.

Has it moved to your elbow?
Has it moved to your neck?

You shout back

It's looking for someone else!

Denise Low

Squaw Pass

High on the pass
the sky comes to an edge,
cuts cruelly deep
then skips upon a ledge
and in its course
begins a valley-dropping glide
that stops the breath
and seems to end in suicide.

John R. Milton

Stopped On Highway 19 West of Redwood Falls

Not a weed left standing
in all of Southwest Minnesota
and not even the memory
of bluestem—Just look
at the rows of newly-planted corn
stretching a green perfection
over miles of flat black soil
Feel the pull of the land
reaching up   to the roadside
to the White Scandinavian need
to subdue   to the whistle-clean
farm yards   red painted barns
holsteins   sausage feeds   quiet
little country towns. Every store
has a special   on happiness
Every field   is a rich
reflection of the nest.
Certainly nothing like Dakota
with its drought and wind and
squalid prairie towns—and rats
you haven't seen rats   until
you've been to Dakota. Given a
choice   even God wouldn't live
there—and who knows   maybe he doesn't
But here   there is safety   in
estimated yields   precision rainfall
and a clean predictable Earth.
Farmers know it. Fourwheeling across
their land   they smile   and wave
from plastic capsules   their faith
like heat waves   rising.

Kevin Woster